CONVERSION

Key Words in Jewish Studies

SERIES EDITORS

Deborah Dash Moore, University of Michigan
Jonathan Boyarin, Cornell University

I. Andrew Bush, *Jewish Studies*
II. Barbara E. Mann, *Space and Place in Jewish Studies*
III. Olga Litvak, *Haskalah: The Romantic Movement in Judaism*
IV. Jonathan Boyarin, *Jewish Families*
V. Jeffrey Shandler, *Shtetl*
VI. Noam Pianko, *Jewish Peoplehood: An American Innovation*
VII. Deborah E. Lipstadt, *Holocaust: An American Understanding*
VIII. Cynthia M. Baker, *Jew*
IX. Daniel Boyarin, *Judaism: The Genealogy of a Modern Notion*
X. Derek J. Penslar, *Zionism: An Emotional State*
XI. Ari Y. Kelman, *Jewish Education*
XII. Miriam Bodian, *Conversion*

CONVERSION

MIRIAM BODIAN

RUTGERS UNIVERSITY PRESS
New Brunswick, Camden, and Newark, New Jersey
London and Oxford

Rutgers University Press is a department of Rutgers, The State University of New Jersey, one of the leading public research universities in the nation. By publishing worldwide, it furthers the University's mission of dedication to excellence in teaching, scholarship, research, and clinical care.

Library of Congress Cataloging-in-Publication Data
Names: Bodian, Miriam, 1948– author.
Title: Conversion / Miriam Bodian.
Description: New Brunswick, New Jersey: Rutgers University Press, [2025] |
Series: Key words in jewish studies | Includes bibliographical references and index.
Identifiers: LCCN 2025005035 (print) | LCCN 2025005036 (ebook) | ISBN 9781978834989 (paperback) | ISBN 9781978834996 (hardcover) | ISBN 9781978835009 (epub) | ISBN 9781978835016 (pdf)
Subjects: LCSH: Conversion. | Conversion—Biblical teaching | Rabbinical literature—History and criticism.
Classification: LCC BL639 .B63 2025 (print) | LCC BL639 (ebook) | DDC 296.7/14—dc23/eng/20250206
LC record available at https://lccn.loc.gov/2025005035
LC ebook record available at https://lccn.loc.gov/2025005036

A British Cataloging-in-Publication record for this book is available from the British Library.

∞ The paper used in this publication meets the requirements of the American National Standard for Information Sciences—Permanence of Paper for Printed Library Materials, ANSI Z39.48-1992.

rutgersuniversitypress.org

Contents

Foreword

The Rutgers book series Key Words in Jewish Studies seeks to introduce students and scholars alike to vigorous developments in the field by exploring its terms. These words and phrases reference important concepts, issues, practices, events, and circumstances. But terms also refer to standards, even to preconditions; they patrol the boundaries of the field of Jewish Studies. This series aims to transform outsiders into insiders and let insiders gain new perspectives on usages, some of which shift even as we apply them.

Key words mutate through repetition, suppression, amplification, and competitive sharing. Jewish Studies finds itself attending to such processes in the context of an academic milieu where terms are frequently repurposed. Diaspora offers an example of an ancient word, one with a specific Jewish resonance, which has traveled into new regions and usage. Such terms migrate from the religious milieu of Jewish learning to the secular environment of universities, from Jewish community discussion to arenas of academic discourse, from political debates to intellectual arguments and back again. As these key words travel, they acquire additional meanings even as they occasionally shed long-established connotations. On occasion, key words can become so politicized that they serve as accusations. The sociopolitical concept of assimilation, for example, when turned into a term—assimilationist—describing an advocate of the process among Jews, became an epithet hurled by political opponents struggling for the mantle of authority in Jewish communities.

When approached dispassionately, key words provide analytical leverage to expand debate in Jewish Studies. Some key words will be familiar from long use, and yet they may have gained new valences, attracting or repelling other terms in contemporary discussion. But there are prominent terms in Jewish culture whose key lies in a particular understanding of prior usage. Terms of the past may bolster claims to continuity in the present while newly minted language sometimes disguises deep connections reaching back into history. Attention must be paid as well to the transmigration of key words among Jewish languages—especially Hebrew, Yiddish, and Ladino—and among languages used by Jews, knitting connections even while highlighting distinctions.

An exploration of the current state of Jewish Studies through its key words highlights some interconnections often only glimpsed and holds out the prospect of a reorganization of Jewish knowledge. Key words act as magnets and attract a nexus of ideas and arguments as well as related terms into their orbits.

This series plunges into several of these intersecting constellations, providing a path from past to present.

The volumes in the series share a common organization. They open with a first section, Terms of Debate, which defines the key word as it developed over the course of Jewish history. Allied concepts and traditional terms appear here as well. The second section, State of the Question, analyzes contemporary debates in scholarship and popular venues, especially for those key words that have crossed over into popular culture. The final section, In a New Key, explicitly addresses contemporary culture and future possibilities for understanding the key word.

To decipher key words is to learn the varied languages of Jewish Studies at points of intersection between academic disciplines and wider spheres of culture. The series, then, does not seek to consolidate and narrow a particular critical lexicon. Its purpose is to question, not to canonize, and to invite readers to sample the debate and ferment of an exciting field of study.

Deborah Dash Moore
Jonathan Boyarin
Series Coeditors

Preface

Although this is not a personal book, it has a personal aspect—one that I hope has enriched its contents. My first acquaintance with Jewish conversion came with the sudden discovery in adolescence that my father's family was Jewish, a fact that had been kept entirely hidden. My father had been baptized, presumably at some point before he married my non-Jewish mother (I never learned the details). Until this discovery, I had considered myself to be "like everyone else" in my environment—neighbors, tradespeople, schoolmates, teachers, store employees, and so on. Given the secrecy surrounding the family's past I preferred to leave it buried. Only years later, after I graduated from college, did I begin exploring the Jewish world. In time, when that world already felt like my own, I underwent *giyyur.*

This set of personal experiences has unquestionably been a factor in determining my path as a scholar of Jewish history. Issues around the changing of socioreligious affiliation—whether by an individual or a group—have been a thread running through much of my work. For most of my career I have dealt with psychic and identity issues among the early modern population of conversos (forcibly converted Jews and their descendants) in Iberian lands, as well as ex-conversos and their descendants who settled outside those lands. The Spanish and Portuguese Jews who were forcibly baptized between 1391 and 1497 were not "converts" in any ordinary sense—certainly not those who continued to hold onto Jewish beliefs and practices. Over time, many but not all the conversos assimilated to Catholicism in what might be regarded as a gradual process of conversion. Yet among assimilated conversos there were those who, impelled by extraordinarily circumstances, converted "back" to their ancestral religion as they conceived of it. (In certain remarkable cases Iberian Gentiles also converted to the "Law of Moses.") But even the most committed crypto-Jews had little inkling of the normative Judaism of their day. Those who escaped to "lands of freedom" were thus compelled to come to terms in one way or another with rabbinic Judaism, undergoing a process that was yet another instance of "conversion."

As rich and varied as these cases of conversion might be, they comprise only a small and atypical cluster of episodes over the long course of Jewish history. Charting the course of "conversion" in its various iterations over the centuries has required a deep plunge into fields far from my own, as well as difficult decisions about what to include or exclude. I would like to thank all those who helped me navigate unfamiliar territory, whether in person or via electronic communications: David Ellenson, z"l, Adam Ferziger, David Golinkin, Sarit Kattan Grivetz, Ephraim Kanarfogel, Daniel Schwartz, Craig Perry, Paola Tartakoff, Anne Oravetz Albert, Shaul (Seth) Farber, Nicole Maor, Jonathan Sarna, Jack Wertheimer, and Moshe Yagur. I am grateful to the staff of the National Library of Israel in Jerusalem for their help, especially during a period of transition as the library was moving to its new quarters.

CONVERSION

Introduction

When the editors of the series Key Words in Jewish Studies approached me about writing a book on the term "conversion," my first impulse was to ask, "What do you have in mind? Conversion *in* or conversion *out*?" The editors, in a liberal spirit, left that for me to decide, and I will get to that decision shortly. But I soon realized that this question was related to an even more basic question: Is there any coherence at all to the term "conversion" as it is variously used in Jewish Studies (or more generally in the orbit of Jewish life)?

The term derives from the Latin verb *convertere,* meaning to turn about. Its use in relation to religious experience has medieval Christian roots. In fourteenth-century Europe it could mean several things: the act of entering a monastery, a spiritual awakening (that is, a turn to Christ), or the institutionalized act of baptism. Thus, even from a very early period, "conversion" had multiple meanings—meanings that, as Karl Morrison noted, were "all cobbled together in an ensemble, or repertory, that enabled writers of twelfth-century Europe to explore, interpret, and explain transformations in their world and in themselves."[1] But as different as the phenomena thus labeled might be, they were all tied to Christian belief and practice.

The classic pioneering studies in modern scholarship on conversion, those of William James (1902) and (relying on James) Arthur Nock (1933), reflected the authors' own culture-bound sensibilities and assumptions. For James, who described what he believed to be a universal psychology of religious conversion, the convert underwent a profound psychic transformation: It could be defined as what happens when "a self hitherto divided, and consciously wrong, inferior and unhappy, becomes unified and consciously right, superior and happy, in consequence of its firmer hold upon religious realities."[2] The limitations of such a subjective, personal, thoroughly spiritual (and decidedly Protestant) conceptualization of conversion have long been noted.

Well before James and Nock put their mark on the study of conversion, nineteenth-century scholars of the Wissenschaft des Judentums movement (literally, the "Science of Judaism," the earliest phase of Jewish Studies) dealt with conversion to and from Judaism from their own decidedly Jewish perspective. Working outside a European academic establishment that was permeated with anti-Jewish biases, they were committed to correcting the hostile representation of Jews and Judaism in mainstream European scholarship. Yet they used the available concepts in the European languages in which they worked. Thus,

Heinrich Graetz used the German equivalents of the English word "conversion" (*Bekehrung, Konvertierung*) whether he was referring to the conversion of Saul of Tarsus to Christianity, the conversion of the Frankish deacon Bodo to Judaism, or the mass forced conversion of Spanish Jews to Catholicism.[3] To be sure, Graetz's Jewish perspective was never in doubt. When he referred to a historical figure in less neutral terms as an *"Apostat,"* it would not have occurred to his readers to imagine that he was referring to a Gentile.

For about a century after its origins, modern scholarship in Jewish Studies developed mainly within the walls of Jewish institutions. Scholars worked in milieus in which they felt little need to contend with the very different phenomena covered by the term "conversion" in other cultural contexts. For the most part, scholars ignored what happened to converts after they entered or left the Jewish community: Those individuals had completed their role on the stage of history. (The exceptions were apostates who polemicized against Judaism and forcibly converted Jews who sustained a crypto-Jewish life.) However, from the late 1970s onward, the insularity of Jewish Studies was challenged both from within and without as it moved into mainstream institutions of higher learning, particularly in the United States. It was around this time that identity theory drew attention to the complexities of religious and ethnic boundary crossing, and Jewish Studies scholars were quick to take note.

In our own globalized academic climate, it is all but impossible to adhere to any fixed, universal conception of "conversion." Collected volumes on the topic of conversion offer an assortment of cases, each presented in its specific cultural, theological, and historical context.[4] What holds these volumes together is the conviction that "conversion" is a useful category for thinking about how cultures and individuals deal with their own or others' passage from one religious orbit to another. Yet there is also skepticism about the usefulness of so pliable a term. The multitude of motivations, rituals, historical situations, and meanings lumped under the rubric "conversion" have led some scholars to question whether it has any meaning at all. Given the impossibility of pinning down a clear, unified conception of the term, Lewis Rambo, a leading figure in conversion studies, stated starkly that conversion is "what a faith group *says* it is."[5] But this formulation, too, has a serious pitfall, because it assumes that members of a given faith group all think about conversion in the same way.

Although, by definition, a book about Jewish "conversion" does not deal with conversion in non-Jewish contexts, the topic is still daunting in its complexity. Jews and Gentiles have moved in and out of each other's religious cultures in manifold ways over the centuries. There is, to be sure, a common thread that runs through this story of conversion, at least from late antiquity onward: the reliance on a set of rabbinic ideas and practices that have proved durable despite controversy and the winds of historical change. Yet even within a given historical moment, the term "conversion" as Jewish Studies scholars use it accommodates phenomena that are situationally and structurally profoundly different. If we are studying, say, the Jews of sixteenth-century Venice, that term has been applied both to the willing baptism of aspiring Jewish printers and to the ritual circumcisions of recently arrived Portuguese conversos. Similarly, in German lands around the turn of the twentieth century, it has been applied both to the radical embrace of Jewishness by the assimilated Jew Franz Rosenzweig and to the baptism of the assimilated Jew Gustav Mahler.

Here we can discern a problem that arises precisely from the modern academic universalization of the term "conversion." A Jew who converts "out" is, from a neutral, flattened dictionary perspective, doing the same thing as a non-Jew who converts "in." Yet if we are interested in how these acts were understood and interpreted within Jewish societies—and that is an aim of this book—we need to recognize that for most of history Jews have not associated these acts in any significant way.

It occurred to me to ask, early in the project, how one might title this book if it were translated into Hebrew. Technically, there is a modern, value-free Hebrew equivalent of the word "conversion" that is used in Hebrew-language scholarship: *hamarat ha-dat* ("change of religion"). But historically this term was not neutral at all. The term *mumar*—someone who underwent *hamarat ha-dat*—was used only for an apostate from Judaism, with all the negative connotations that entailed. The lack of a single term for "conversion" in classical Hebrew hints at a deep-seated semantic differentiation in Hebrew between a Jew's apostasy, on the one hand, and a Gentile's adoption of Judaism, on the other. In Jewish texts (certainly in premodern ones), as well as in much of common discourse today, the act of a Gentile who becomes a Jew and the act of a Jew who rejects Judaism for another belief and way of life are unrelated—linguistically, conceptually, and affectively.

Let us consider the relevant set of Hebrew terms. First, an apostate from Judaism is called a *meshumad*, a pejorative term derived from the root *shemad*, connoting "destruction." (*Mumar* is a less harsh alternative.[6]) For decades, scholars of Jewish Studies reinforced the existing conceptual chasm between conversion out of Judaism and conversion into Judaism by maintaining that a Jew's act of apostasy involved an exit from Jewish history, making it of little interest.[7] Yet, although Jews have generally considered a *meshumad* to be a defector, they do not regard him as having become a Gentile (*goy* or *nochri*). Consider the famous rabbinic dictum about the Jewish apostate: "A Jew, though he has sinned [through apostasy], remains a Jew."[8] However, the matter is not quite so simple, and certain converted Jews *can* in effect become non-Jews (or something very close to it), according to both rabbinic and secular Israeli law.[9]

More importantly, apostates are never mere individual actors: They are acting within a certain environment. Jews who undergo baptism, for example, do not thereby extricate themselves from the fraught, complex world of

Jewish–Christian relations. The church's special targeting of Jews for evangelization, as part of its struggle to eliminate troublesome Jewish challenges to its interpretation of the Hebrew Bible, paradoxically makes Jewish baptism a very Jewish story. More broadly, diaspora Jews have in many times and places been exposed to pressures to convert to the dominant religion, making acts of apostasy—and the subsequent fate of the apostates—intrinsic elements of a larger Jewish story.

A second Hebrew term for "convert" is *ger*, a rabbinic term for the voluntary convert to Judaism. (That the biblical term *ger* does *not* mean "convert" will be discussed; suffice it to note here that the Hebrew Bible has no specific term for a Gentile who joins the Jewish community and adopts Jewish practices and beliefs). In the postbiblical sense, *ger* has both positive and negative associations. The sincere convert (*ger tzedek*) merits a special blessing in the foundational daily Hebrew prayer.[10] This might seem to imply a generally favorable Jewish attitude toward converts to Judaism. Such an impression is reinforced by the fact that the sympathetic figure of Ruth the Moabite (to whom we shall return) has long been regarded as the archetypal *ger*. Yet the qualified term *ger tzedek* in the prayer—that is, *sincere* convert—implies the existence of other kinds of *gerim*; indeed, rabbinic texts are not invariably enthusiastic about Gentiles who have become Jews.

A third type of convert in traditional Jewish taxonomy is the *anus* (pronounced *ah-noose′*). This is a Jew (literally, "a forced one") who has been compelled under pressure or threat of death to convert to another religion—most often Christianity but also Islam. Such persons have occupied an ambiguous position within the Jewish world unless they chose and were able to return fully to normative Jewish life. Because coerced conversion has at certain junctures been a major aspect of Jewish experience, it too falls firmly within the bounds of the key word "conversion" in Judaic research.

One might ask whether any coherent analytic framework can be developed that justifies treating these forms of conversion together in a single work. To be sure, all acts of conversion involve boundary crossing, and the motivations of *meshumadim* and *gerim* may overlap. For example, both the apostate and the *ger* may have primarily spiritual motivations, both may convert because they wish to intermarry, or both may be seeking social acceptance, and so on. But is it useful to use the inclusive modern neutral concept of "conversion" to think about Jewish experience over several millennia?

I have tried in this short volume to consider conversion as broadly as possible as an act of socioreligious boundary crossing. It charts how, across the long arc of Jewish history from biblical times to the present, patterns of boundary crossing—whether of Gentiles entering Jewish life or Jews exiting from it—have developed and shifted. It analyzes how these patterns have been shaped by the various human ecosystems involved and highlights both continuities and discontinuities. It does not seek to impose conceptual coherence on the diverse phenomena examined.

Although there are many works dealing with Jewish conversion, there is no accessible book-length study that can serve as an overview of and introduction to the topic. I hope that this book, although far from exhaustive, will provide that point of departure. For scholars who are engaged in examining Jewish conversion in specific times and places, it may suggest a more capacious framework for analysis. For nonspecialists, it provides a brief, accessible introduction to a sweeping topic.

Let me lay out the contours of the book. Part I surveys the history of conversion in the Jewish orbit from the biblical period to the establishment of the State of Israel.

We begin with an examination of the biblical text—not primarily as a historical document but as a source that was used by future generations to think about the relationship of Jews and Gentiles and the possibility of crossing the boundaries that separated them. Fundamental to that thinking were the biblical conception of the origins of the Jewish people in God's covenant with Abraham and the repeated exhortation to the Children of Israel to distinguish themselves from Gentiles through their observance of the Torah (or "Law") revealed at Mt. Sinai. Yet the foundational Torah text—the Hebrew Bible—raised innumerable questions. Could a person who was not descended from Jacob become an Israelite by declaring loyalty to the God of Israel? What exactly was the status of foreigners (*gerim*) who lived under Israelite rule? And given the many biblical examples of marriages between Israelite men and foreign women, what lay behind the decree of Ezra-Nehemiah (fifth century B.C.E.) not only prohibiting such marriages but also sending away foreign wives and their children?

The late Second Temple period in Palestine (second century B.C.E.–70 C.E.) saw significant new developments. By the time the Hasmonean rulers threw off Seleucid (Greek) imperial rule and asserted Jewish sovereignty—a victory that future generations would commemorate by celebrating Hanukkah—Palestinian society had absorbed much of the Hellenistic culture that held sway in the eastern Mediterranean. It was under Hellenistic influence that Gentiles were incorporated into the Judean polity with the requirement that they adhere to Jewish law and custom; they thus became fellow Judeans. More important in the long run was the fact that by the first century C.E., individual Gentile converts, referred to as "proselytes" in Greek and Latin sources, were a recognized presence in Jewish society.

Yet it was only in the rabbinic period (first through sixth centuries C.E.) that a process of formal conversion—*giyyur*—was formulated. Scholars differ as to when rabbinic law became the normative mode of Jewish life in Palestine and Babylonia. But it was in the early centuries of the Common Era that the learned teachers first known as "rabbis" laid the foundations for the legal and homiletic corpus that would govern Jewish life for centuries, in texts known as the Mishnah and Talmud. The key features of the conversion process they instituted were the supervision of each case by a *beit din* (rabbinic court), the immersion of the convert in a ritual bath, circumcision (for males), and the convert's acceptance of the commandments of the Torah as interpreted by the rabbis. Even though the *ger* was declared to be a Jew in every respect, the rabbis qualified this status in certain specific ways.

By the medieval period, rabbinic law had become normative throughout the Jewish world, which had developed new centers in northern Europe, Spain, and North Africa. Yet *giyyur* remained mainly a matter for Jews to *think* about, because under Christianity and Islam, with their powerful systems of religious control and indoctrination, few Gentiles converted to Judaism (except for emancipated slaves). Given the conditions of Jewish life, it was Jews, not Gentiles, who were most likely to change their religion, whether persuaded by polemics or pressured by circumstances. In rabbinic law such persons remained Jews, although with some alterations of status. Of course, Jews were sometimes baptized or islamized against their will, usually during episodes of popular religious violence. Until the late medieval period, such converts were often able to return to the Jewish community. The trail of those who did not was quickly lost. The case of late medieval Spain and Portugal was exceptional. There, under the surveillance of the Inquisition, the descendants of large numbers of forcibly converted Jews became a distinct population that included both sincere Catholics and crypto-Jews; although baptized at birth, they continued to be labeled "converts" (*conversos*)—a term that took on a quasi-racial meaning.

With the rapid spread of Protestantism in the sixteenth century, Europe entered into the profound upheaval known as the Reformation. In northern Europe, the breakdown of church authority made possible the emergence of various new forms of Christianity. Echoes were felt in the Jewish orbit, particularly in the community of ex-conversos in Amsterdam where, in a sign of things to come, some Jews openly challenged traditional rabbinic authority. Yet for the most part, being a Jew continued to mean living in a Jewish community under rabbinic supervision. The universal acceptance in this period of a code of Jewish law known as the *Shulkhan Arukh*, which aimed to standardize Jewish practice throughout the diaspora, reaffirmed classic rabbinic rulings—including those on *giyyur* and on the status of apostates.

The modern period brought major and rather sudden disruptions to traditional patterns of life that produced significant changes in the way boundaries were crossed. With the emergence of modern states committed to principles of religious freedom, with the legal emancipation of Jews, the opening up of new opportunities, and the attractions of a secular outlook, Jews loosened their ties to Jewish communal life or abandoned it altogether. In a society that placed a high value on individual freedom, a Jew could let go of every aspect of Jewish identity without joining another religious community. Yet it was not uncommon for Jews to apostatize, usually to marry a non-Jew or to overcome professional and social barriers. High rates of intermarriage produced a sense of crisis and highlighted issues around *giyyur* as never before. Jewish law had long held that the wish to marry a Jew was not a valid motivation for conversion, yet increasing rates of intermarriage threatened Jewish survival. Did these new circumstances require a rethinking of traditional rulings? Different responses to the crisis of modernity led to a fracturing of rabbinic leadership and a reorganization of Jewish communal life along new lines, giving rise to today's Orthodox, Reform, and Conservative streams. The different requirements for *giyyur* among these streams led to an unprecedented situation in which a conversion performed according to the standards of one rabbinic authority or court was not recognized by another, raising issues about the boundaries of Jewishness and theoretically posing the threat of schism.

Part II of the book explores the conflicts and controversies around conversion in the Jewish world in the postwar period. The issues have been most contentious in Israel, where tensions are built into the very structures of government. The 1950 Law of Return, originally enacted to ensure the right of all Jews to settle in Israel as citizens, was broadened in later decades to include non-Jewish children and spouses of Jews, as well as converts to Judaism from the three major streams. However, in matters governed by the Chief Rabbinate, which include marriage, burial, and conversion, much stricter standards of Orthodox halakha were applied to determine a person's religious status. The chief problem this has created is the untenable status of a population of about a half-million immigrants and their children from the Former Soviet Union who participate fully in Jewish Israeli life as citizens according to the Law of Return but are classified as Gentiles by the Chief Rabbinate.

Very different conditions from those in Israel prevailed in the postwar diaspora, causing very different issues around conversion. For the sake of simplicity I focus on American Jewry, by far the largest and most influential diaspora community. Unlike in Israel where the state plays a regulatory role, in the United States conversion to Judaism is a matter between an individual and a Jewish community of their choosing. High rates of intermarriage have given rabbis and rabbinic courts a strong incentive to ease the way for potential converts. Yet, the lack of agreement among the major streams about what constitutes a valid conversion have heightened concerns about the possibility of schism. Efforts were made to introduce a path to conversion that would be acceptable to the three major denominations, but they were not successful. Adding to the lack of clarity about the boundaries of identity, increasing numbers of young Americans have turned their backs on organized religion, seeking a spiritual home in Jewish Renewal groups and other radically individualized (and often commercialized) modes of religious community whose adherents insist on personal, subjective definitions of identity.

There is also a globalized dimension to Jewish conversion, one that has drawn the attention of scholars in recent decades. With modern travel and communications, Jews and Jewish organizations have made connections to groups scattered across the globe that have been isolated from mainstream Jewish life for generations or that, in some cases, have only recently developed beliefs about their Jewish roots. The Jewish Agency, among other interested parties, has been involved in efforts to bring about the formal conversion and immigration to Israel of members of these "emerging Jews," as some scholars refer to them. The beliefs and practices of the Ethiopian Jews or the Bnei Menashe of India, among others, challenge the traditional stark binary of Jew/Gentile and have led rabbinic authorities to rule in sometimes contradictory ways on whether conversion (or at least a modified form of conversion) is required for them to be accepted fully as Jews.

Finally, in Part III, the book examines recent developments in research on Jewish conversion. As the general field of conversion studies has gained traction in recent years, Jewish Studies scholars have been invited to contribute to edited volumes that bring together investigations of religious conversion across a variety of cultures. Such collections bring attention to what is anomalous and worthy of special attention in Jewish life while stimulating insights about common underlying themes. Yet making accurate comparisons has proved to be a challenge, given the diversity of pathways by which people enter or leave religious communities. I briefly discuss an area in which genuinely productive comparative work has been done in a society—late medieval and early modern Spain—where both Jews and Muslims were forcibly converted and where the Inquisition provided unparalleled documentation.

Part III further explores how scholars have integrated insights about identity formation into their study of conversion. Conversion, of course, always involves a change in identity. Ruth's declaration of her intention to make Naomi's people and God her own has long symbolized such a transformation in Jewish popular consciousness. However, contemporary concepts of identity have shifted scholars' focus from the public act of adopting a new religion to the mental work of internalizing new modes of living and thinking. Especially since the 1990s scholars have explored Jewish conversion with a heightened sensitivity to the fluidity, contingency, and uncertainty of identity in general and of the convert's identity specifically. Finally, Part III suggests several areas that call out for further study.

The structure of this book adheres to the guidelines for the volumes in this series. It is not—and is not intended to be—a work with a single core argument about Jewish conversion. Indeed, it demonstrates the futility of such an aim. Rather, the book aims to excavate an extensive scholarly literature on the rich realms of experience so often casually compressed into the term "conversion."

PART I

TERMS OF THE DEBATE

1 Biblical Period

Our starting point is an examination of what the biblical text has to say (or not) about "conversion." The approach is necessarily two-pronged. On the one hand, the Hebrew Bible is the foundational text of an ongoing religious tradition, in both its mythic and legal aspects. On the other, it is a key source (or set of sources) for understanding ancient Israelite history. In this chapter I point to major scholarly insights about how and when non-Israelites were able to join the Israelite *ethnos* and about how the biblical text relates to such instances, with their implications for later generations.

The Hebrew Bible located the very origins of the Jewish people in an act of conversion. It was an act that defied normal patterns of behavior in ancient Near Eastern societies, where a person's consciousness of self was inseparable from their ties to kin, ethnic group, and cult. The idea of choosing to abandon one's roots in order to adhere to a foreign cult seems to have been virtually unimaginable. Yet in biblical and rabbinic sources, Abraham is viewed as having done just that—or rather something *like* that, since he chose not to join a different existing cult but to abandon the entire world of existing cults.

Yet if Abraham did the unthinkable, leaving behind his country, his kin, and his father's house (see Gen. 12:1) for a set of beliefs unknown to his ancestors, Scripture relates that he did so in partnership with God, making his conversion a singular act: It was clearly not intended as a model for anyone else. On the contrary, Abraham's covenant with God obligated his descendants to honor and perpetuate that same covenant. Compliance with this task was central to consolidating the anomalous new identity of Abraham's descendants (through Jacob) and distinguishing them from idolatrous peoples. The importance of maintaining this boundary was such that God commanded the Israelites entering the Land of Israel to smite the Canaanite peoples, destroy their idols, and refrain from intermarriage with them so that they would remain a "holy people" unlike "all the [other] peoples on earth" (Deut. 7:1–6). The boundaries of the *ethnos*, on the one hand, and the community of worshippers, on the other, were at least rhetorically identical. The norm was clear: Ancestry (at least through the male line) determined who was an Israelite and, as such, a worshipper of the one God.

In its descriptive and narrative passages, however, the Hebrew Bible offers a more complex picture. It is obvious even from a superficial reading that ancient Israel included persons whose ancestry was not traceable back to Jacob.

This was true at the very inception of Israel's history as a people: The mixed multitude that accompanied the Israelites out of Egypt (Ex. 12:38) was assimilated without any apparent difficulty or opposition. This was, however, an exceptional moment, and for the most part the absorption of these ancestral foreigners had little impact on Jewish historical consciousness.

Jews today often innocently assume that the biblical "*gerim*" were, quite simply, converts to "Judaism." This identification has had apologetic and polemical value. It offers the reassuring image of a Jewish people that always welcomed outsiders. As such it serves to rebut accusations of Jewish chauvinism and insularity. But the automatic identification of the biblical "*gerim*" with proselytes is grounded in a misunderstanding—albeit an understandable one, given that for the last two millennia the term "ger" has indeed meant "Jewish convert."

Although the biblical text itself nowhere suggests an act or process of conversion by which a person of non-Israelite origin could became an Israelite, this does not mean that assimilation or partial assimilation did not take place.[1] Scholars have long tangled with the question of what the category "*ger*" (or "*ger toshav*") actually meant in the various biblical sources in which it appears.[2] There is general agreement that the *ger*, or "sojourner," was a member of a minority ethnic group who (unlike the "*nokhri*") did not have a foreign homeland somewhere else. But biblical scholars continue to debate the legal, social, and religious characteristics of the biblical *ger*. Although we will not explore the complexities of that debate, some general observations are in order.

In some passages of the Pentateuch, the term "*ger*" simply means a person—any person—living in a foreign land, with all the vulnerability that such a situation implied: The *ger* was a helpless outsider who deserved compassion and aid. In this sense the term might be used both for a non-Israelite living among Israelites and for an Israelite living among non-Israelites. Abraham, seeking a burial place for his wife Sarah in Hebron, said to the natives, "I am a stranger and a sojourner (*ger ve-toshav*) with you" (Gen. 23:4). Moses, sojourning in Midian, named his son Gershom because, he said, "I have been a stranger (*ger*) in a strange land" (Ex. 2:22). The ethnic neutrality of "*ger*," when used in this sense, is underscored by passages that liken the vulnerable non-Israelite *ger* to the vulnerable Israelite *ger*. Thus, the biblical text repeatedly mentions God's command to Israel not to oppress the non-Israelite *ger* because "you"—the Israelites—"were strangers (*gerim*) in the land of Egypt" (Ex. 22:20 and elsewhere). In these passages, outsider status is the very essence of the *ger*'s condition.

Yet other biblical sources represent the *ger* differently, as an ethnic "other" who was nevertheless integrated to some degree into the religious–national life of Israel. The various sources relating to *gerim* in this way raise as many questions as they answer. There is general agreement that before the monarchy, the category of *gerim* referred exclusively to foreigners who settled among the Israelites (and not to indigenous non-Israelites). But what happened under the monarchy? Did this category come to include semi-judaized indigenous peoples? Or descendants of Israelite refugees from the northern kingdom? Or even, perhaps, landless Judahites displaced by Assyrian conquest?

Certainly, there are instances in the Hebrew Bible in which *gerim* are represented not as strangers but as a distinct subpopulation of Israel. They participated in the renewal of the Covenant at Moab (Deut. 29:10–11 and cf. Deut. 31:12) and were exhorted on that occasion to observe the Torah, or biblical law. They could participate in the three pilgrim festivals (Deut. 16:10–14) and bring sacrifices (Num. 15:14–15). Like the Israelite, the *ger* was required to bring a purification offering (*khatat*) for an inadvertent violation of a commandment (Num. 15:27–29) and was subject to *karet* (extirpation) for a willful violation. However, unlike Israelites, *gerim* were permitted to eat ritually unfit meat (Deut. 14:21). Male *gerim* were apparently not required to undergo circumcision to participate in Israelite worship in these ways: indeed, Scripture stipulates that circumcision was required of *gerim* only in one voluntary situation, that of bringing a Passover sacrifice (Ex. 12: 48–49).[3] Yet as time passed it seems likely that like minorities in many societies, a significant number of *gerim* were assimilated into Israelite society and their origins forgotten.

Whatever the ambiguities, the fact that certain biblical passages located *gerim* within the framework of Israelite law and ritual life later provided a hook for the rabbis, facilitating their appropriation of the term "*ger*" to denote something related but essentially new: that is, a religiously committed and ritually introduced convert. The rabbinic "*ger*," unlike the biblical one, was not a stranger or a subcategory of Israel but a person whose legal and social "otherness" was at least theoretically eliminated. Anchoring the innovative institution of rabbinic *giyyur* in biblical language provided the appearance of continuity and camouflaged the degree of novelty it entailed. The rabbis further reinforced the illusion of an unbroken tradition when they projected the essence of rabbinic *giyyur*—that is, an inner transformation of belief and commitment—onto various biblical figures. The "rabbinization" of Ruth the Moabite is but one example of the grander rabbinic project of instilling the notion of a seamless Jewish tradition. Ruth is portrayed, for example, in midrash (an expansive, often boldly imaginative genre of rabbinic exegesis), as being instructed by her Israelite mother-in-law Naomi in practices that were far later rabbinic innovations.[4]

But let us return to the biblical context. Did the marginal status of the biblical *ger* mean that a person of non-Israelite origins living among Israelites could never gain the status of Israelite? As mentioned, it is possible that, under the radar, individual *gerim*—or even groups of non-Israelites—quietly assimilated into the Israelite people by a sort of social osmosis. There is, however, one explicit path by which non-Israelites—at least female non-Israelites—seem to have integrated fully. Even though biblical sources evince disapproval of exogamy, Israelite men sometimes took foreign women as wives. (Technically, women from certain nations were prohibited to Israelites, but this restriction was not adhered to scrupulously.[5]) An Israelite who captured a beautiful foreign woman in battle could also take that woman in marriage (Deut. 21:10–14). Consistent with the patriarchal norms of Israelite society, it would appear that foreign men, unlike foreign women, could not be integrated by marriage.[6] In contrast, foreign wives were expected, as a natural corollary of their marriage, to accommodate to their husbands' form of worship. Their "conversion" (like their marriage) did not entail any prescribed ritual process: It required no declaration of commitment or belief, but only, it would seem, an outward accommodation to Israelite practice. As such, it was a far cry from the sincere and sweeping inner change of heart for which, in rabbinic sources, Abraham's journey became paradigmatic.

Nevertheless, it would be wrong to conclude that the Hebrew Bible lacks instances in which persons of non-Israelite origin were inspired to worship the God of Israel. Let us look at two cases in which a simple reading of Scripture suggests such a change of heart. Without getting into scholarly issues of chronology, language, and historicity, let us consider these cases simply as elements of the biblical corpus. First there is the example of Moses's father-in-law Jethro, a priest of Midian. Jethro was already Moses's father-in-law when he went to meet him in the wilderness and Moses related to him the miracle of the Exodus from Egypt. Moses's report elicited Jethro's expression of awe at the greatness of the God of Israel: "Now I know that the Lord is greater than all gods" (Ex. 18:11). To be sure, this statement falls conspicuously short of being a firm and exclusive commitment to the God of Israel. Still, its significance was immediately recognized and affirmed by a ritual celebration: Jethro brought sacrifices to the God he had just acknowledged as supreme and then participated in a solemn meal attended by Moses, Aharon, and the elders (Ex. 18:12).

More consistent with biblical theology than Jethro's declaration was that of Na'aman, the Aramean commander who journeyed to the kingdom of Israel to be healed from leprosy. After following Elisha's instructions to wash in the Jordan River, Na'aman was cured and responded by making the striking announcement: "Behold, now I know that there is no God in all the earth" except in Israel. He added that he would "henceforth offer neither burnt offering nor sacrifice to other gods, but to the Lord." Na'aman nevertheless remained an ethnic foreigner. Like Jethro, he did not undergo circumcision. He returned to Aram, and although he sought God's pardon, he acknowledged that as a close courtier of the king he would have to bow down to the god of Rimmon (2 Kings 5:15–18).

The Jethro and Na'aman narratives may stand out as biblical examples of "conversion" to those who are looking for such examples; however, when seen in context they have a different thrust. Both Jethro and Na'aman were men of authority in their own cultures. (This is especially emphasized with Na'aman, "captain of the host of the king of Aram" and "highly esteemed" [2 Kings 5:1]). As leadership figures they commanded respect. Moses listened to and followed Jethro's political advice. Na'aman, seeking a cure, went straight to the king of Israel with a letter of introduction from the Aramean king. The declarations of Jethro and Na'aman thus offered valuable "objective" and external affirmation of the greatness of the God of Israel. However, these men did not become Israelites. After their dramatic "conversions," both returned to their homelands (Jethro, before the revelation at Mt. Sinai), never to be heard from again.

We are left, then, with the assimilation or naturalization of foreign women as the closest thing to "conversion" in the Hebrew Bible. Its acceptability was reinforced by a tradition of patrilineal descent that rendered the mother's background more or less inconsequential. Even if the wife was never fully assimilated, her children would be. It is true that the biblical text (prior to Ezra and Nehemiah) tells us nothing explicit about the status of the children of a foreign mother—but biblical narratives suggest that having a foreign mother presented no impediment to a child. The sons of Joseph and his foreign wife Asenath were each granted the exceptional privilege of founding a tribe of Israel. The descendants of Ruth the Moabite included King David and other rulers of Judah. To be sure, the children of foreign wives would have been especially vulnerable to the possibly idolatrous influence of their mothers, but that did not alter their Israelite status.

Despite expressions of disapproval, nothing in the pre-exilic period suggested that the practice of intermarriage with foreign women might have had within it the seeds to produce a crisis. But the upheavals of the sixth century B.C.E. transformed the traditional order. The decline and destruction of the kingdom of Judah, the creation of a Babylonian diaspora, and the return to Jerusalem of Babylonian exiles under Persian rule provided the backdrop to the turmoil described in Ezra-Nehemiah. According to this text, with its many difficulties,[7] when Ezra arrived in Jerusalem with a group of returning exiles (referred to as "*b'nei ha-golah*"), he discovered that previously arrived exiles (including descendants of the high priest Joshua) had intermarried with local women and had made themselves at home in an idolatrous environment (Ezra 9:1–4).[8] He took the extraordinary step of ordering these foreign wives and their children to be divorced from their husbands and expelled from the community. He did not make allowances for them, nor did he offer them the option of "converting" (so one might imagine) by undergoing instruction and committing exclusively to the God of Israel.[9]

Ezra's draconian step may have been an emergency measure, a deviation necessitated by extraordinary circumstances. Yet the text of Ezra-Nehemiah does not present it that way. It portrays this measure as entirely consistent with traditional Torah teaching, supporting its claims with somewhat manipulated Pentateuchal sources.[10] Israel was the "holy seed" (*zera kodesh*) and as such was to be kept absolutely separate from the profane seed of the Gentiles. Scholars continue to debate what kind or kinds of purity—ritual, "moral," or genealogical—were meant in the Ezran discourse of purity. The debate is understandable given that the text does not offer a consistent, systematic ideology but instead relies on an array of biblical sources drawn from various contexts to lay out what is in fact a novel vision of Israelite identity.

The singular priority given to genealogical purity in Ezra-Nehemiah is reflected in the lengthy genealogical lists of the *b'nei ha-golah*—lists that placed the returning exiles in a separate category from the intermarried "Israelitish" population they encountered. A secondary but important factor affirming the Ezran claim that the exiles were the true heirs to the Torah was their experience of exile and return, one that made them the true successors of the Israelites who left Egypt. With these two criteria, the ancestral and the experiential, Ezra-Nehemiah justified the exclusion of the many other inhabitants of Judea who identified with the biblical Israelites and the Temple. (The latter are referred to as the "people of the land" [*amei ha-aratzoth*], a term that denies them any clear identity.) It was the *b'nei ha-golah* alone who constituted the true community of Israel; only they could lead a sanctified existence. This inflexible new vision of the covenantal community precluded anything even faintly resembling "conversion." It should be noted, however, that we know next to nothing about the degree to which the policy as laid down was actually implemented. In any case, the unbending exclusivity of the Ezran outlook did not inform what would become mainstream.[11]

2 Second Temple

The history of Judea in the four centuries from the time of Ezra and Nehemiah to the Hasmonean revolt—that is, from the sixth to second centuries B.C.E.—is quite obscure. In this brief chapter I focus on the period of ferment from the second century B.C.E. to the destruction of the temple in Jerusalem in 70 C.E. It is true that an Ezran-like concept of genealogical purity—one that excluded from the Jewish community persons who were not of the "holy seed"—survived into the Hellenistic and early Roman periods, at least in certain circles (among them, the Jewish sectarians of Qumran).[1] Yet this perspective was but one strand (and by no means the most prominent) of a complex tangle of Second Temple perspectives about the nature of the Jews (or "Judeans," a term scholars prefer for this period) and about whether (or how) a Gentile could become a Judean (*Ioudaios*).[2]

As we have noted, in the biblical Near East a person's identity was immutably bound up with family and clan, and the notion of an independently aware and motivated self was inconceivable. Members of one ethnic group might allow their own ancestral world of myth, custom, and memory to mingle with a foreign one (as occurred repeatedly with the Israelites), but they did not "join another religion." They did not, that is, adopt a system of belief that transcended local, ethnic, and customary loyalties. It is not that Israelite belief lacked transcendent elements. There was, above all, the principle of the unity of God. But in general, the preservation of that transcendent principle was seen as the exclusive obligation of the descendants of Jacob, and Gentiles were seen as posing an at times almost existential threat to it.

If we fast-forward to the Hellenistic period, we find a dramatically changed environment. When the Macedonian Greeks conquered the eastern Mediterranean in the fourth century B.C.E., their conquered territories were exposed to, and became permeated with, an imperial culture that transcended local customary experience. Greek language and literature, as well as Greek material culture, generated a profound cultural reorientation among the inhabitants of a vast region. Among other things, acculturation to Greek culture instilled an attitude of condescension to the local and particularistic. Other ethnic cultures were generalized and collectively devalued as "barbarian," because they shared the lamentable characteristic of not being "Greek." But a barbarian could *become* a "Greek" by adopting a Hellenistic way of life—something that did not preclude maintaining ancestral loyalties as well.

In such an environment one might imagine that just as a barbarian could become a Greek, so too could a Gentile become a Judean. And indeed, the Hasmoneans seem to have implemented a policy that echoed the Greek model of subject-population assimilation. As the Hasmonean state expanded by conquest, significant numbers of Gentiles were incorporated into the Judean polity and were required to adhere to Jewish law and custom.[3] The Hasmonean policy entailed an implicit reconceptualization of what it meant to be a "Judean": It became a kind of citizenship that entailed adherence to the Torah. Although it did not lose its ethnic underpinnings, it could also exist independently of them.[4]

The incorporated populations included Idumeans and Itureans, both with long-standing ties to the Judeans. (Herod, the infamous king of Judea under Roman rule, was a descendant of Idumeans who became Judeans in this way.[5]) The Idumeans and Itureans were pressured to conform to Judean law and custom and changed their behaviors accordingly, bowing to the political reality. The reluctant were "encouraged" to conform by being threatened with expulsion if they did not.[6] These converts occupied an anomalous position—Josephus referred to Herod as "an Idumean, a half-Jew"—but they were not formally relegated to an inferior social or religious category.[7] And their origins were eventually forgotten. The fact that the Hasmonean elite was not troubled by its own policy—one that was so at odds with biblical admonitions—would seem to reflect, among other things, prevailing cultural winds in a hellenized eastern Mediterranean world.[8]

By the first century C.E., literary sources and inscriptions reveal instances of conversion that can be said to anticipate rabbinic *giyyur*, in which the convert was required to accept the exclusive God of Israel and the practice of Jewish laws (including circumcision). Gentile authors Tacitus and Juvenal, as well as Jewish authors Philo and Josephus, all attest to individual Gentiles who thus became Jews, whom they referred to in Greek and Latin as "proselytes."[9] Ossuary inscriptions from Rome, Jerusalem, and elsewhere supply concrete evidence of the existence of such converts. The twenty-some deceased persons whose names appear on these inscriptions were referred to in Greek as "the proselyte" or in Hebrew or Aramaic as "the *ger*." Either way, the qualifier functioned as a kind of patronymic in place of what would normally have been the father's name.[10] Such inscriptions say all too little about who the converts were or what led them to become proselytes. We can surmise, however, that Second Temple prophetic, apocalyptic, and wisdom texts that emphasized justice and righteousness and identified the Torah with wisdom (without, to be sure, abandoning themes of national chosenness and Temple worship) echoed a wider elite Jewish culture, one that was expressed in a language intelligible and even attractive to non-Jews. Something like a Jewish "religion," a creed and practice that one could adopt by choice, was emerging.

3 *Rabbinic*

It would be hard to overstate the transformation in how a Gentile became a Jew that was brought about by the scholars of the Mishnah and Talmud: These texts revolutionized the way the biblical text was approached. The Mishnah, compiled in the early third century, was a foundational collection of rabbinic debates; between the third and eighth centuries, they were extensively elaborated in what became the Talmud. The Babylonian version of the Talmud, the "Bavli," became the central text of rabbinic Judaism and the primary source of Jewish religious law (*halakha*).[1]

Curiously, the rabbis' early elaboration of *giyyur* took place in a period when Jewish life might be thought to have lost its appeal to Gentiles; it was in the wake of the destruction of the Temple in 70 C.E. when the community was suffering under increasingly oppressive Roman imperial rule. Scholars disagree about the degree to which a demoralized Jewish population may have accommodated to Roman domination, to the point of being paganized.[2] But it seems unsurprising that there is meager evidence for conversion to Judaism in the rabbinic period from the destruction of the Temple to the Muslim conquests of the early seventh century. We know of only a few converts in Babylonia where Jews also lived. More cases are mentioned in Palestinian sources, among them prominent figures like R. Meir, R. Akiva (descended from converts), and Shemaya and Avtalion, teachers of the great sage Hillel. But nowhere is there evidence of widespread conversion.[3]

It is also striking that *giyyur* was an innovation ordained by a small cadre of rabbis whose authority in late antiquity seemed to have been quite modest.[4] However, neither the scarcity of actual candidates for conversion nor the rabbis' own limited influence deterred them from ambitiously reconceiving the terms on which Gentiles might be absorbed into the Jewish people (or, if found wanting, turned away). They relied for their authority on their mastery of the sacred texts, their guardianship of the oral teachings of generations of scholars, and their creative energy. They viewed themselves as heirs to an intellectual and spiritual tradition that reached back to Moses. And to some extent they filled a vacuum after the destruction of the Second Temple when the priesthood was left decimated and, later, when the patriarchate, after a period of considerable power, suffered a precipitous fall.

It is true that the issue of *giyyur* occupied only a trifling place, quantitatively speaking, in the talmudic corpus. But it was a vital component of an all-encompassing effort to reestablish Jewish existence on the basis of rabbinic rulings, halakha. Yet, however new the rabbis' program, it would be a mistake to regard rabbinic *giyyur* as pure innovation. The mishnaic rabbis seem to have taken for granted the practice of "*giyyur*." The term crops up in the Mishnah without explication. It discusses, for example, the case of a Jew suspected of relations with a Gentile woman who "subsequently converted [*nitgiyyera*]"—no elucidation was evidently needed for the term.[5] This lack of explanation hints at the significant legacy of the Second Temple period. Important as the developments of earlier centuries were, they yielded practices and perspectives that were radically different from place to place. The rabbis, although justly famous for their lack of agreement on almost any given issue, established basic norms that were in time to form the backbone of Jewish existence in the diaspora. This does not mean that they left the kind of record scholars would wish for. Despite the extensive efforts of scholars to understand the rabbinic corpus historically, uncertainty remains about how halakhic opinions evolved—when, where, and in what context they were articulated—and how textual difficulties should be understood. Here, I describe the basic lines of early rabbinic thinking about *giyyur*.

When a Gentile approached a rabbi to undergo conversion (and in rabbinic texts this is how the conversion process invariably began), it would be incumbent on the rabbi (or rabbis) to evaluate the potential convert's motivations. The worthy convert was one who sought to convert "for the sake of heaven" (*l'shem shamayyim*). Rabbinic sources did not discuss what exactly this phrase meant.[6] They did, however, enumerate, in a typically suggestive, telegraphic style, what they regarded as unacceptable motivations for conversion: (a) the wish to marry a Jew, (b) the fear of Jews (exemplified by the so-called lion converts of 2 Kings 17, as well as "the converts of Mordecai and Esther" mentioned in Esther 8:17), (c) the expectation of material benefit ("for the sake of a royal table"), and (d) the hope of gaining prestige ("for the sake of joining Solomon's servants").[7] The rabbis agreed that sincere, religiously motivated converts should be accepted, but they differed about how to respond to the others. Some held that *giyyur* should not be performed at all when the motivation was not "for the sake of heaven." Others, however, held that, although not ideal, worldly motivations should not preclude conversion.

In general, once performed, *giyyur* was considered irreversible. If a convert willfully violated halakha, he or she would not revert to being a Gentile but would be deemed a Jewish apostate (*meshumad*).[8] It is important to note, however, that there was an opposing, lone opinion about the irreversibility of conversion. Rav Nehemiah held that if "unkosher" motivations came to light after *giyyur* had already been performed, such a discovery would render the conversion invalid ex post facto.[9] But the predominant opinion was that rabbinic authorities could not revoke a properly conducted *giyyur*. This did not mean that the ritual act effected some kind of inherent, immutable transformation of the person who underwent conversion. *Giyyur* was a contractual undertaking, not a transfiguration. This is evident in the prevailing rabbinic opinion, which is still the norm, that Gentiles converted as children could reject and annul their conversion when they reached adulthood.[10]

The classic description of the conversion ceremony appears in the talmudic tractate Yevamot.[11] The theoretical convert presented here (unsurprisingly a male) is first warned of the hardships life as a Jew might entail. An anonymous "they" (presumably the rabbis) are instructed to ask why he wants to convert, given that "Israel at this time is pained, oppressed, harassed, and torn, and that afflictions come upon them." If the potential convert is undeterred by this grim assessment—the ideal response is given as the rather opaque, "I know and am unworthy"—the rabbis proceed to make known to him "a few of the light commandments and a few of the severe commandments." They inform the convert that by undergoing *giyyur* he is subjecting himself to the possibility of severe punishments for actions that would previously have been permitted to him, for example, profaning the Sabbath. At the same time, they inform him of the rewards for fulfilling the commandments. "But they do not speak too much to him," the Bavli advises, "nor are they too detailed with him." If the convert accepts the terms laid out to him, "they circumcise him immediately."[12] Once the convert is healed from the circumcision he is immersed. During his immersion he is again instructed in "a few of the light commandments and a few of the severe commandments." Here, for the first time, the text specifies who "they" are: namely, "two rabbis." After this the convert is "like an Israelite in all respects."

This marks the end of the procedure for the generic convert. But it is not the end of the passage in question, which continues, "[In the case of] a woman, women [attendants] have her sit in water up to her neck, and two disciples of the sages stand near her outside [the bath] and make known to her a few of the light commandments and a few of the severe commandments." The brevity of the description of female *giyyur* should not belie its significance. Immersion as part of the conversion process was just emerging in the early rabbinic period. The fact that female converts were required to undergo a rite of passage at all was an innovation.[13] Circumcision had long served as the rite for male Gentiles entering the Jewish community, but there had been no act marking the entry of Gentile women. That such a ritual was felt to be missing is reflected in a pointed passage in which the Bavli asks, "From what source do we derive that our ancestral mothers underwent immersion when they received the Torah at Mount Sinai?" The Bavli's droll reply: It was a logical necessity because if they did not immerse, what act would have brought them under the wings of the Divine Presence?[14] Conversion without a ritual act validating it had become unthinkable. Whatever its actual immediate impact in practice, the introduction of immersion spelled the impending end of a social reality in which a Gentile woman's conversion was essentially a byproduct of marriage to a Jew. With immersion, female converts were recognized as independent actors whose will and state of mind mattered.

Yet although *giyyur* was equally available to men and women, the gender differences in the process were obvious. The designation of circumcision as one of the two ritual requirements for conversion—indeed the crucial one, according to some textual traditions—was highly significant. Circumcision was not only a surgical procedure but also a powerful symbolic marker of Jewishness, representing entry into the covenant between God and the Children of Israel. For this reason, even a circumcised Gentile male was required to undergo a symbolic circumcision (*hatafat dam*). The marginalization of female converts that this entailed was underscored by the fact that the only ritual women underwent—immersion—had no such meaning.[15]

The passage in Yevamot covers an additional category of convert: the emancipated Canaanite slave. The procedure could not be stated more briefly: "The same law applies to the proselyte and to the emancipated slave."[16] The slave had already attained a liminal status somewhere between Jew and Gentile at the time he or she was acquired. Male slaves were circumcised, and all slaves were obligated to observe certain halakhot. As the talmudic rabbi R. Hisda put it, the slave "has left the category of Gentiles but has not yet entered the category of Israelite."[17] On emancipation, a slave "entered the category of Israelite" by undergoing immersion and accepting the commandments like all proselytes. The freed slaves' agreement was technically required for this to occur. But by the time of their emancipation, they would have been conditioned to the ritual life, language, and customs of their Jewish community and, presumably having few options, would continue to be part of the only community they knew. Although freed slaves, like foreign-born wives, were prohibited from marrying into the priestly caste, there is no indication that their offspring were restricted in any way.

During the same period when the rabbis laid out the basic requirements for *giyyur*, they also, in an understated way, introduced a dramatic and anthropologically intriguing innovation with important implications for conversion: They replaced a deeply ingrained patrilineal principle with a matrilineal one, admittedly with some inconsistencies.[18] Just why this happened, given that the patrilineal model prevailed up to the late Second Temple period, is a mystery.[19] This is not the place to enumerate the various theories. For our discussion here, what matters is that the determination of identity through the maternal line, along with the requirement of ritual conversion for Gentile women as a condition for marriage to a Jewish man, gave female converts and their children a newly clarified status. The rabbis could not have imagined the many implications of this principle for a later era when endogamy was no longer the rule in Jewish life.

Let us return to the delineation of a conversion process. The passage in Yevamot laid out a procedure that was finalized by the physical act of immersion. Yet it made clear that it was not circumcision or immersion but rather acceptance of the Torah's commandments that was the essence of *giyyur.* It underscored this requirement by including a "teaching moment" in the conversion ritual itself. As mentioned earlier, the convert was to be instructed in "a few of the light commandments and a few of the severe commandments." In addition, he was to be taught some quite particular laws: "And they make known to him the sin of violating the laws of the gleanings, the forgotten sheaf, the corner of the field, and the poor tithe"—the obligation in the Land of Israel to leave certain portions of one's crops to the poor. Although the reason for specifying these halakhot is a matter of speculation, Avi Sagi and Zvi Zohar suggest that the aim was to instill in the convert an understanding that joining the Jewish people was "not primarily a vehicle to personal religious salvation" but also involved important social and economic commitments.[20]

In this passage and others, the rabbis placed conversion on a new footing, defining the convert as a person entering not just an ethnic community but also a normative religious domain defined by halakha. Implicit in the new articulation of conversion was a shifting conceptualization of Jewish identity itself. If what made someone a Jew was knowledge of and commitment to Torah, the convert needed first and foremost to go to school. This image of the convert appears in the famous tale of the Gentile who said to Hillel, "Convert me, on condition that you teach me the whole Torah while I stand on one foot." Hillel complied, but he then directed the neophyte to "go study."[21] He demonstrably refrained, however, from holding the convert immediately responsible for the full weight of halakhic observance. As we have seen, the passage in Yevamot also discouraged making overly burdensome demands on the convert's capacities. Yet there were those rabbis who took a more severe view. Passages in several different sources contain the dictum that a convert who "took upon himself all the words of the Torah *except one*" was not to be accepted.[22] Such an impossibly demanding standard surely reflected a rabbinic stylistic tendency to underscore a point by exaggeration, but it served to emphasize the core value of Torah commitment.

Increasingly, conversion was to be solemnized with formal rabbinic oversight. The stipulation in the Yevamot passage that "two rabbis" must be present for the final immersion of the male convert constituted a recognition of a supervisory rabbinic role: There is no mention of such a role in mishnaic sources. According to one scholar on the subject, the tannaitic sources "generally assume that conversion is performed by the converting Gentile himself—with no requirement for the participation of other Jews."[23] It is in talmudic sources that we first find the requirement of a rabbinic court, most importantly in the ruling of Rabbi Yehuda that "a potential convert who converts before a court is a valid convert, whereas if he converts in private, he is not a convert."[24] Validation of conversion by a *beit din* of three became the norm toward the end of the talmudic period.[25]

The shift of emphasis from the genealogical toward the normative-religious made it possible to declare that the newly minted convert was "like an Israelite in every respect" or, in a different passage, that a convert "was like a newborn babe."[26] Such categorical statements did not mean that the convert's Gentile past had no bearing on his or her status. Overall, there was no such category as simply "an Israelite in every respect." Hierarchical structures had always existed in Jewish life; social organization in antiquity was unthinkable without them, and the convert's place in the social structure of Jewish antiquity was quite evidently inferior. What the phrase "like an Israelite in every respect" meant was that, with conversion, a Gentile irrevocably crossed the line separating Gentile from Jew. Thus, the convert did not occupy some kind of middle ground and could not return to his or her previous status. Similarly, the statement that a convert was "like a newborn babe" did not mean that a convert's origins were somehow eradicated. Its context was a narrow and specific one: A male convert who had fathered sons when he was a Gentile was a "newborn babe" in the sense that the first son born to him after his conversion was deemed a halakhic "firstborn" (*bekhor*).[27]

What consequences, then, did the convert's prior life as a Gentile have for his or her life as a Jew? Let us look at two discrete areas where one's Gentile background mattered. First, in the area of marriage, a female convert was prohibited from marrying a priest (*kohen*).[28] This had to do with the complex realm of rabbinic thinking about purity and impurity, the profane and the sacred. The rabbis, who sustained the biblical concern for the purity of the priestly lineage, regarded the female convert as retaining something of the profaneness of the Gentile. This blemish put her in the category of other Jewish women whose blemishes rendered them unfit to marry into the priesthood—among them divorcees, emancipated slaves, and women degraded by illicit sexual unions.[29] Some rabbis extended the prohibition to the *daughter* of a convert, but the prevailing opinion was that the indefinable profaneness that derived from one's Gentile background disappeared in the second generation.[30]

A quite different sort of debate about the convert's status developed around a liturgical and theological issue. The question was whether a convert who lacked any Jewish ancestry could address God in prayer as the "God of *our* fathers, God of Abraham, God of Isaac, and God of Jacob," given that the convert's fathers were pagans. A similar issue was raised about the formula a Jew was to recite when he brought first fruits to the Temple (Deut. 26:3), in which he declared that God had sworn to "our fathers" to give "us" the land. Given the verbal fastidiousness of the rabbis, it is not surprising that they would be concerned about the propriety of a convert's making these statements. The Mishnah held that a convert who lacked Jewish lineage was not permitted to recite the prescribed declaration when he brought first fruits. Concerning the Amidah prayer, the central prayer of the Jewish liturgy, the Mishnah held that the convert was to modify the standard formula: When he prayed alone, rather than saying "God of our fathers" as stipulated in the liturgy, he was to say "God of *the fathers of Israel*," and when he prayed with the community he was to say "God of *your* fathers."[31] The Babylonian Talmud supported this position.[32]

The Jerusalem Talmud, however, which even though it was ultimately eclipsed by the Babylonian Talmud had its own place in the tradition, categorically rejected this approach. R. Judah held that a convert should address God like any other Jew as the "God of our fathers," based on a verse in Genesis in which God, elucidating the meaning of Abraham's new name, declared, "I have made you the father of a multitude of nations [*av hamon goyim*]" (Gen. 17:5). R. Judah interpreted the verse thus: "In the past you were a father to Aram, but now, henceforth, you are a father to all the nations"—a mode of paternity that clearly was not biological and that, understood spiritually, rendered converts his descendants.[33]

The notion of Abraham as the progenitor of converts was made yet more explicit in midrash. The biblical hook on which to hang this claim was the verse according to which Abraham's household, on the journey to the Land of Israel, was accompanied by "the souls they [Avram and Sarai] had made in Haran" (Gen 12:5). What did it mean, the midrash asked, to "make" souls? It meant that Avram and Sarai had created converts through proselytizing. Again, the representation of Abraham as both a spiritually and biologically generative figure reflected a shifting conceptualization of Jewish identity, one in which shared religious values provided the foundation for community.[34]

The image of Abraham and Sarah reaching out to Gentiles, effectively converting them and bringing them along on a journey to a distant land, seems to reflect a quite positive view of *giyyur* and of a proselytizing impulse that is generally absent in halakhic discourse. Rabbinic literature routinely refers to *giyyur* using a poetic metaphor that is associated with active persuasion on the part of Jews: The convert is "brought" under the "wings of the *Shekhina* [Divine Presence]."[35] A midrashic passage enjoins all Jews to seek to convert Gentiles "just as Abraham prevailed upon those around him and brought them under the wings of the Divine Presence."[36] The desirability of converts could be discerned even in God's plan for Jewish exile. According to Rabbi Elazar, "God scattered Israel among the nations for the sole purpose that proselytes should be numerous among them."[37]

In such passages, Gentile converts are welcome, but they are shadowy, disembodied figures who scarcely seem to play a role in their own conversion. A more dynamic image of the convert appears in the story of three Gentiles who came before Shammai and Hillel—major scholars of the Mishnah who represented different schools of thought—to request conversion. Each of the Gentiles posed conditions for their *giyyur* that led Shammai to summarily reject them. Hillel, in contrast, undertook to educate and guide them. The three converts, successfully indoctrinated, expressed their gratitude to Hillel, whose patience "brought us beneath the wings of the Divine Presence."[38] Implicit in the story is the Gentiles' coming to terms with the requirements of *giyyur*, with help from Hillel but ultimately through their own efforts.

The rabbinic model par excellence of the active, self-directed convert was Ruth the Moabite. Even in the unvarnished biblical text, Ruth appears as a full-blown personality, the driving force behind a drama that unfolds with pathos. She spurns what would have seemed conventional behavior, first when she rejected Naomi's efforts to discourage her from accompanying her and then when she accepted Naomi's plan to unite her with Boaz. She is the only convert (or "convert") in the Bible whose boundary crossing is marked by a full-throated declaration of commitment to the Israelite people and their God.

Ruth's exemplary behavior in the biblical story was further elaborated by the rabbis. Notable in their development of the story was the imposition of a rabbinic model of conversion, with Torah learning at its core. Naomi was granted a quasi-rabbinic supervisory role, and Ruth, rather than proclaiming her own conversion as the biblical text would have it, was transformed into an eager student. The Midrash accomplished this alteration by taking Ruth's words of commitment and turning them into a set of responses during Naomi's halakhic tutorial. Ruth's statement, "Where you go, I shall go," became a response to Naomi's directive that one must not go beyond the prescribed Shabbat limit (*techum ha-shabbat*). (Or alternatively, that it was "not the way of Israelite women to go to theaters and circuses of the Gentiles.") When Ruth said, "Where you lodge, I shall lodge," it was in response to Naomi's instruction that she should not improperly spend time alone with a man (or, alternatively, reside in a house where there was no *mezuzah*). When Ruth said, "Your people are my people," it was in response to Naomi's instruction that Jews observed 613 commandments.[39]

The favorable representations of Ruth notwithstanding, it would be a mistake to imagine that the rabbis always entertained favorable views of converts. The corpus of early rabbinic texts can perhaps best be viewed as a stockpile of ideas, attitudes, and interpretations from which future generations could selectively draw. The range of thinking and opinion about *giyyur* and *gerim* was accordingly broad. At one end of the spectrum are the hyperbolic statements about the excellence of converts. According to Resh Lakish, for example, a proselyte was more precious in God's eyes than the Israelites at Mt. Sinai. Why was this? Because without the thunder, the flames, the lightning, the quaking of the mountain, and the sound of the rams' horns, the Israelites would not have accepted the yoke of the Torah, whereas the convert came forward to accept that yoke without any great pyrotechnic display.[40] According to another rabbinic tradition, the souls of all future converts, along with those of all future born Jews, were present at Mt. Sinai.[41] At least rhetorically, even descendants of the blackest villains of Israelite history—the genocidal Persian courtier Haman, the Canaanite general who oppressed the Israelites for two decades, and the Assyrian king who lay siege to Jerusalem—could become model Jews. "Some of Haman's descendants studied Torah in Bnei Brak," a passage in the Bavli declared, "and some of Sisera's descendants taught children Torah in Jerusalem, and some of Sennacherib's descendants taught Torah in public"—including Shemaya and Avtalyon, Hillel's teachers.[42]

At the other end of the spectrum are sources that view converts in a starkly negative light. A much-quoted statement in that vein can be found in the key passage from Yevamot discussed earlier. That passage, you may recall, required that the potential convert be given an opportunity to withdraw. Why was it a good idea to offer such an opportunity? Because, in the words of R. Helbo, "converts are as harmful to the Jewish people as a leprous scab on the skin."[43] The same unpleasant image was deployed again in the same tractate, together with a contrived reading of Proverbs 11:15, bending that verse to mean "evil after evil will come to those who accept converts."[44] In a well-known passage, the great medieval commentator Rashi drew on midrash to hold the "mixed multitude" who left Egypt with the Israelites—identified explicitly as *gerim*—responsible for fashioning the golden calf.[45] Elsewhere the mixed multitude are associated with every imaginable evil, the implication being that their Gentile ancestry inclined them to such behavior.[46]

We have no evidence of the actual social realities faced by converts during the formative period of rabbinic thinking about *giyyur*. Yet rabbinic measures to protect the dignity of converts from insults presumably reflected a response to actual incidents. Invoking the biblical injunction against oppressing the *ger*, Jews were prohibited from reminding the convert of his or her origins. As one passage vividly warned, "You should not say to [the *ger*], 'Last night you were worshipping Baal, Kores, and Nebo [Isaiah 46:1] and you had pork between your teeth, and you dare to speak words against me?'"[47]

Conclusion

The *ger* emerged in the Second Temple period as a figure who was no longer merely a naturalized foreigner absorbed into a genealogically rooted Jewish family but rather an individual who actively chose to join the Jewish community and commit to its way of life. Such a development was made possible by the emergence in late antiquity of something like what we think of as "religion"—that is, a sphere of human activity that dealt with the divine and that was not necessarily organically connected to one's ethnicity, ancestral cult, or land of birth. Early rabbinic texts formalized and regulated the reception of Gentiles into the Jewish community. They also laid the foundations for future rulings and deliberations around the subject of *giyyur*. Yet conversion clearly had dimensions that were not fully expressed in law. The mythic and theological conceptualization of *giyyur* in early rabbinic literature, where the *ger* was represented variously as being an heir of Abraham, as accepting the yoke of the Sinaitic covenant, or as taking refuge under the wings of the Divine Presence, was essential for anchoring the phenomenon of conversion into a broader Jewish metaphysical vision.

4 *Medieval*

The medieval period, from about the seventh to fifteenth centuries, saw the creation of a profoundly new setting for Jewish understandings of "conversion." The parameters of Jewish identity were now more or less uniform throughout the diaspora. Under the leadership of the *geonim*, the heads of the Babylonian academies (*yeshivot*) whose influence from the eighth to eleventh centuries extended throughout the Jewish diaspora, the Babylonian Talmud became authoritative, except among the Karaites.[1] This gave Jews a well-defined identity with clear boundaries, distinguishing them from the Gentiles among whom they lived. Whether in Fustat, Damascus, Saragossa, or Wurms, a Gentile conversion to Judaism had similar features.

However, the conceptual contours of *giyyur* in a world dominated by Gentiles had changed. At least until Christianity became a significant force in the Mediterranean, conversion was a uniquely Jewish phenomenon: A Gentile could convert to Judaism, but there existed no phenomenon of conversion to a Gentile way of life, with a ritual act that expressed exclusive commitment and personal religious choice. By the medieval period this had changed decisively. Jews lived among populations, whether Christian or Muslim, that had literally come into being through a process of formalized individual conversion.

It is, of course, problematic to generalize about so vast and complex a geohistorical entity as "the medieval world." But if one feature characterized the situation of the Jews over the course of nearly a millennium, from the breakup of the western Roman Empire to the rise of Atlantic trade, it was their subjection to the rule of two monotheistic religions with universal claims. The exclusivity of those claims contrasted with the relatively open style of Hellenistic and Roman cultures. At least among the clergy, an ethos of theological absolutism prevailed. The influence of the clergy, supported by (and integral to) imperial, royal, and provincial governments, translated into enormous power over minds. One can still feel an echo of that power, expressed in massive stonework and vaulting arches, when one enters a medieval cathedral or mosque.

A Jewish minority was mostly tolerated under Muslim and Christian rule, even though Jews were removed from entire regions by expulsion. In places where Jews were allowed to reside, authorities took measures to ensure that they appeared defeated and worthy of contempt, lest they present an attractive religious alternative. Jews were subjected to discrimination, heavy taxation, stigmatization, and, at times, violence. They were portrayed as immoral and, especially by the late medieval period, as dangerous; this image served to corroborate the claim that their understanding of the Word of God was a willful falsification. For those Gentiles who overcame the psychological and practical barriers to *giyyur*, there was a further catch: Conversion from the dominant religion to Judaism was a crime punishable by death (at least in theory), both in Christendom and Islam. Yet such conversions did occasionally take place, under the supervision of rabbis whose authority as the gatekeepers for entry into the community was unquestioned.

It is true that there were periods of relatively good relations and even mutually enriching coexistence among Jews and non-Jews. This has been underscored by recent generations of scholars as they have challenged what the Jewish historian Salo Baron famously called the "lachrymose conception of Jewish history." Yet however lively the interactions may have been, the underlying assumptions did not support anything resembling modern religious toleration. Appreciating the religious "other" was never a value in the medieval orbit. Indeed, righteousness and divine justice were invoked by both Christian and Muslim authorities to justify not only "mild" measures of discriminatory legislation but also violent crusades. Under these conditions, it is not surprising that medieval conversion to Judaism was a rare occurrence and that the commonest form of "conversion" involving Jews was Jewish apostasy, or *shemad*. In certain periods, Jews also suffered forcible conversion (*ohnes*); entire Jewish communities sometimes submitted under violence (or the threat thereof) to Christianity or Islam.

The concept of apostasy was not new to Jewish thinking. The terms *mumar* and *meshumad* had early rabbinic origins. However, the medieval shift in socioreligious structures gave these interchangeable terms new meaning. In talmudic literature they had the meaning of "habitual sinner"—that is, a person who consistently violated halakha.[2] As the early rabbis envisioned it, such a person might have one of two motivations for his behavior. He sinned either "from appetite" (*letayavon*) or "to express insolence" (*lehahkis*)—for example, either because he liked the taste of pork or because he enjoyed openly flouting the prohibition of eating it.[3] What the talmudic rabbis did not envision was a habitual violation of the Torah motivated by the *mumar*'s abandonment of Judaism for another exclusive ideology/theology.

Medieval apostates were taking just such a step—something that, value judgments aside, was analogous to *giyyur* in that it entailed formal and exclusive acceptance of a different religious tradition. Such behavior raised fundamental questions. Was a Jew who converted in this way untethered from the obligations of the covenant? Did Christian or Muslim rituals of conversion, performed on Jews, have standing from a Jewish point of view? If so, did the apostate become a Gentile? Did it matter whether the conversion was voluntary or coerced? Could Jewish apostates return to Judaism, and if so, did they need to undergo some type of "deconversion" to return to the fold?

The towering eleventh-century religious authorities Rashi and Rabbenu Tam held that apostates, despite their formal abandonment of Jewish tradition and communal life, did not lose their underlying identity and status as Jews.[4] Their rulings reflected a wish to keep the door open for apostates who might choose to return to the Jewish community—as quite a few did. Rabbinic scholars of later generations, however, expressed a wider range of views about the status of apostates. They often supported a ritual act—immersion—to mark the return of the apostate to the Jewish community, thus implicitly distinguishing the *meshumad* from other Jews. Still, the *meshumad* was never regarded as a non-Jew; indeed, halakhists sometimes explicitly distinguished the immersion of the returning apostate from that of the *ger*.[5]

Medieval halakhic discussions are important sources of information about apostasy, but, as with *giyyur*, the dense and demanding arguments of rabbinic discourse, rooted in a particularistic legal tradition, were removed from the fierce medieval polemical battleground where the convert/apostate was both an actor and a subject acted on. Despite their relatively small numbers, their powerlessness, and the fact that they generally desisted from proselytizing, Jews remained a significant presence on that battleground because they possessed scriptures that were foundational to both Christianity and Islam. The question of the true interpretation of these scriptures was at the heart of medieval polemics and played a role in both *giyyur* and apostasy. Any discussion of medieval Jewish "conversion" would thus be incomplete without some consideration of the competitive spiritual milieu.

Although this might seem like the moment to turn to major developments in the Muslim and Christian orbits, one important digression is in order: It deals with a medieval episode that unfolded in a pagan environment. It would seem to be one of the least likely episodes of *giyyur* in Jewish history and has long fascinated scholars and laypeople alike.

Khazars

This anomalous episode occurred during the early period of Christian and Muslim expansion, between the eighth and tenth centuries. It began with the conversion to Judaism of the rulers of the central Asian kingdom of Khazaria, followed by the conversion of many of their subjects. The Khazars were a nomadic, pagan Turkish people about whom little is known. Scholars have scratched their heads for decades seeking to reconstruct why and how these conversions took place. One author commented, "A reasonably limited body of evidence coupled with extremely high interest has meant that almost every plausible—and implausible—argument and counterargument that can be drawn from the sources has already been drawn."[6]

The episode is best known to Jewish readers from the poet/philosopher Yehudah Halevi's work the *Kuzari*, written in Arabic in 1140. In this work the king of the Khazars, seeking enlightenment, hosts a scholarly debate between a Jew, a Muslim, and a Christian. He ultimately chooses to convert to Judaism. The *Kuzari* occupies an unquestioned place as a classic of Jewish philosophy and theology. However, if we want to consider what really happened in the steppes of Khazaria in the eighth century, it is best to set it aside. It was written centuries after the events in question. Halevi may have had access to tenth-century Hebrew sources, including a purported reply of the Khazar King Joseph to the Jewish scholar and diplomat Hasdai ibn Shaprut. Yet the accuracy and authenticity of these documents, like other sources touching on the Khazar conversions, are in doubt. In any case, Halevi was not primarily interested in the Khazar conversions at all. His king of the Khazars was a literary creation, a device to prompt a theological/philosophical debate with the aim of reinforcing the Jewish loyalties of his readers.

The warrior nomads of Khazaria, we can safely assume, had a limited interest in the fine points of theology or philosophy. What we do know about their native religious practices is consistent with other Turkic pagan rituals, including human sacrifice. Grave sites of the Khazar nobility show that they placed a high value on military prowess: The sites were decorated with images of naked warriors in ritual combat, wearing masks and carrying spears. Archaeological excavation shows that wild boars were sacrificed at sacred oak trees.[7] In light of the evidence, scholars agree that the factors at work impelling the Khazars to convert to text-based monotheistic religions (some Khazars also converted to Islam and Christianity) are to be found in places Yehudah Halevi did not explore.

Certainly nothing about these conversions fits the rabbinic model of *giyyur* developed in late antiquity, in which Gentiles came before a Jewish court as individuals to formally commit to the practice of halakha. Although a great deal about the Khazar conversions remains hidden from view, the adoption of some form of Judaism by the Khazar elite fits a broader pattern: that of nomadic steppe peoples opting, during a phase of state-building, for one or another of the universal religious systems that sedentary cultures had developed. In these instances, the conversion of elites almost always preceded more widespread conversions in the general population. Scholars have sought to understand the politics of such conversions—and the gradual, shaky transition from pagan practices to the new religion—by examining conversions in other Turkic cultures in this period, whether to Christianity, Islam, Buddhism, or Manichaeanism.[8]

It is mainly a matter of conjecture why the Khazar rulers turned specifically to Judaism, especially because Judaism, unlike Islam or Christianity, lacked a strong proselytizing impulse. The prevailing explanation is that, caught between the mutually hostile, expanding powers of Christian Byzantium and Islam, these rulers saw Judaism as a neutral religious system that would help sustain their independence. Commerce may also have played a role: Given that Jewish merchants dominated trading between Europe and Asia, the Khazar rulers may have seen conversion to Judaism as offering mercantile advantages. One scholar has argued that it was probably Jewish traders known as Radhanites, whose routes passed through Khazar lands, who introduced Khazars to a form of Judaism, "present[ing] their beliefs in a popularized version attractive to people unaccustomed to theological abstractions."[9] Some Khazars may also have learned about Judaism from the Jewish emigres who entered Khazaria after fleeing persecution in Byzantium or after leaving the Muslim caliphate. According to another hypothesis, a Khazar ruler who figures in some sources came from one of the Jewish communities on the Black Sea; his military successes as a commander led to his becoming a de facto ruler of the Khazars.[10]

Whatever specific factors were involved, clearly the conversion of Khazars to Judaism took place gradually and did not result from a dramatic mass spiritual movement. In any case, the episode was short-lived: The Khazar Jews disappeared in the tenth century when their kingdom was absorbed into the Islamic world.

The conversion of the Khazars, although an enduring source of fascination for scholars and history buffs alike, was a minor chapter in the lengthy story of medieval Jewish history. It was in the lands under Muslim and Christian rule that Jewish life developed in ways that would have an enduring impact. We first examine developments in the Muslim Mediterranean and Near East, because in the early medieval period virtually all Jews lived under Islam.

Under Islam

Freed Slaves

The most common form of *giyyur* in Islamic lands is one that, as we have seen, was already prescribed in the Talmud: It was effected partially when a slave entered a Jewish household and was completed when they were manumitted.[11] Domestic slavery was a fact of social life in the wealthy urban centers of the Muslim world, and in this respect, as in others, Jews were no different than their Muslim neighbors. Rabbinic law stipulated that when slaves were purchased they were integrated into a Jewish home through a process that had elements of *giyyur.* This meant circumcision for male slaves, ritual immersion for slaves of both sexes, and acceptance of the halakhot for which they were obligated in carrying out their duties. Rabbinic authorities differed on whether confirmation by a *beit din* was necessary. They also differed on whether a slave needed to willingly accept circumcision, immersion, and acceptance of the relevant halakhot. All agreed, however, that a slave was not fully a Jew. As the Jewish philosopher Maimonides put it in his *Mishneh Torah*, echoing the Talmud Bavli, "Slaves who have been immersed for the purpose of slavery, and accepted upon themselves those commandments which are incumbent on slaves, are no longer considered Gentiles, but are not yet considered Jews."[12]

The status of slaves changed when they were freed. With the issuing of a certificate of emancipation (*get shikhrur*) and ritual immersion they were granted the full status of a Jew. Thanks to Geniza documents and geonic legal rulings, we have an idea of what that meant in tenth- to thirteenth-century Egypt.[13] Unfortunately, little is known about the origins of the slaves involved so we can form little impression of the conceptual world they inhabited before their capture. Of those slaves mentioned in the Geniza whose origins were at least partially documented, most were Nubian; others were Persian, Indian, Moroccan, and Frankish. Some were Christian, others pagan.[14] (None were Muslim because Jews were not allowed under Islamic law to own Muslim slaves.[15]) We know nothing, however, about how they coped cognitively or spiritually with their new circumstances. Having been torn from their native milieu (unless they were born into slavery) and being entirely subordinate to their masters, they had lost any vital connection to the sources of their preexisting beliefs. We can assume that they continued to think and process their experience in terms that to one degree or another reflected their native cultures. This is a well-documented phenomenon in other historical settings. Inevitably, however, they would have had to adapt to the religious and cultural norms of their masters. Rabbinic authorities discussed (and differed on) the permissibility of holding a slave who refused to accept semi-conversion to Judaism, suggesting that at least occasionally slaves resisted their "judaization."[16] But such cases were clearly the exception.

The great majority of the slaves who appear in the Geniza documents were female. This was because the tasks that domestic slaves performed—caring for children, cleaning, and cooking—were traditionally female tasks. In the course of their work, these slaves were thoroughly conditioned to the rhythms and practices of Jewish life. Presumably this conditioned their thinking as well as they became more familiar with the meanings attached to what they were doing.

The evidence shows that slaves often became deeply enmeshed in Jewish households, both practically and emotionally. A dying mistress in the thirteenth century was moved to say before witnesses that "my slave woman Munā has attended graciously to me during this and previous illnesses in ways that my mother and sister have not done."[17] In this case and others like it, the slave had become what Pierre Bourdieu called "practical kin."[18] This is not to say that relations between slaves and their masters or mistresses were never conflictual—and, of course, slaves were fundamentally property that could be bought and sold.[19] Yet ties of affection and loyalty between Jews and their slaves were not uncommon and played a role in the assimilation of the freed slave to Jewish life.[20]

It has been argued that these ties echoed the patronage relationships typical in medieval Muslim societies, in which both the patron and the protégé had something to gain.[21] For the mistress, the cultivation of a female slave served to extend her kinship network. The slave, in turn, attained a status that was more like a poor cousin than a slave. It was not at all unusual for Jewish masters and mistresses to free their household slaves, often in deathbed wills in which they typically provided material assistance to the propertyless slave. According to one scholar, nearly one-third of the individual slave women documented in the Geniza were freed slaves.[22]

Domestic female slaves were unsurprisingly vulnerable to sexual predation on the part of their masters. Indeed, evidence shows that female slaves who were concubines of their masters constituted a significant subcategory of freed slaves.[23] Strictly speaking, masters who had sex with slaves were in violation of halakha, which prohibited such relations. Indeed, masters were prohibited from marrying a freed slave with whom they had previously had sex. Yet in the social world of the Geniza, the sexual exploitation of slave women seems to have been an unremarkable occurrence. Maimonides, recognizing the social reality, ruled that marriage to a slave concubine was permitted, because it was preferable to maintaining a slave in concubinage.[24]

Conversions that accompanied emancipation were carried out in a rabbinic spirit, if not always strictly according to established halakha. The elements of the actual ceremony are rarely described, but existing evidence suggests that they might typically have included a declaration of commitment to observing halakha, immersion, and the adoption of a Hebrew name. A detailed *get shikhrur* of 1198 describes a ceremony in which the *beit din* first admonished the slave concerning observance of the commandments, after which she immersed in a ritual bath in the synagogue of the Iraqi Jews in Fustat.[25] As mentioned, slave owners typically provided freed slaves with the material means to attain a reputable status in Jewish Egyptian society, which would mean, for newly freed female slaves, the means to marry a member of the community. There is ample evidence that most (though not all) freed slaves remained in the Jewish community and integrated into it without major difficulty. Even if vestiges of their past as slaves might remain for a generation or two—during a quarrel, for example, they might be subjected to insults referencing their slave pasts—their status as full members of the community was secure.[26]

Voluntary Converts

The trajectory of the relatively few voluntary converts to Judaism in the medieval Islamic world is sketchy. Only a handful of halakhic queries sent to rabbinic authorities deal with such *gerim*, and only thirteen documents from the Cairo Geniza offer details about specific cases of *giyyur*.[27] Existing documentation usually omits—whether intentionally or out of indifference to our curiosity—even the most basic information about the converts' religious or geographical background.

Scholars once believed that because Islam prohibited any religious conversion except to Islam, the converts mentioned in the Geniza must all have converted in Christian lands, from which they were then forced to flee. Many cases clearly fit that pattern, and Geniza documents throw vitally important light on them. (We discuss them later.) However, there were exceptions. At least one well-known convert—Ovadiah "the *Ger*," to whom Maimonides famously wrote a letter—is strongly believed to have converted from Islam.[28] And there were clearly others.

We know of the existence of some converts simply because they are mentioned as "so-and-so the *Ger*" in lists found in the Geniza of persons who received material support from the Jewish community in Egypt. ("The *Ger*" was invariably used as a suffix, replacing the convert's patronymic—a symbolic erasure of origins.) Others appear in letters of recommendation that a convert could use to solicit charity. Converts sometimes also petitioned wealthy members of the community on their own, describing their plight. One such indigent convert portrayed himself with literary flair as "the proselyte, your servant Mordekhai, the young, the low, the destitute, the immigrant, the poor, the desolate, the bitter, exiled from my place, detached from my land, like a bird wandering from her nest." Unfortunately, like other petitioners, Mordekhai did not offer any information about his conversion and exile.[29]

The fact that solicitations for charity are such an important source of information about *gerim* can be misleading. The travails and wanderings described in these petitions were not unlike like those of other poverty-stricken persons and should not be taken as a characteristic of converts in general. It is true that integration into the community was not always easy. The many converts who had to uproot themselves from their homes lost their sources of income, forcing them to rely on charity. But more prosperous converts also appear in communal documents.[30] One highly successful convert, Abu al-Khayr "the *Ger*," became a member of the Jewish elite of Fustat in the late eleventh century and was known to have engaged in philanthropic activity himself.[31]

We can only presume that the *gerim* mentioned in the Geniza records underwent a rabbinically prescribed ritual for conversion before a *beit din*. The case that produced the longest and most detailed description of that ritual—in a court deposition of the eleventh or twelfth century—is not at all what one might expect, given the procedure outlined in the talmudic tractate Yevamot. The converts involved were two Christian sisters who, in an unidentified place (not necessarily under Muslim rule), approached some unidentified Jews, declaring that they wanted to abandon all "idolatry and pagan worship," join the Jewish community, and accept "the yoke of the commandments." At first the Jews declined to perform the conversion, but the sisters were insistent, warning that they would "complain to heaven" if their request were denied. What ensued was a ritual borrowed from the biblically prescribed practice for marriage to the "beautiful woman" captured in war (Deut. 21: 10–14, discussed in chapter 1): The sisters were instructed to shave their hair with a razor and cut their nails. They then wept in remorse for having committed idolatry and recited a biblical verse from Jeremiah expressing the Gentiles' eventual repudiation of their ancestors' falsehoods.[32] Only then were they immersed and accepted as converts.[33]

The shaving of hair and paring of nails as part of a postbiblical conversion ritual were not new practices but dated to the early geonic period in Babylonia. Such a ritual was by no means universally practiced—Maimonides did not include it in his code—but it was widely prescribed as late as the sixteenth century.[34] It was apparently extended to another rite of passage as well. The Dominican inquisitor Bernard Gui reported the Jewish practice of shaving the hair and paring the nails of baptized Jews who returned to the Jewish community. Borrowing this custom for returning apostates suggests that the ritual was understood as an act of repentance and purification—a renunciation of a defiling past.[35] As such, it is consistent with the recitation by the two sisters undergoing *giyyur* of a verse that nullified prior false beliefs. Yet both for the *ger* and the returning apostate, the practice might also be understood as symbolizing the effacement of the "old" person and the emergence of the "new," as self-regenerating parts of the body were removed and allowed to grow back.

Perhaps the best-known of the medieval proselytes was Ovadiah "the *Ger*" who sent an inquiry to Maimonides. His question was whether, as someone with no Jewish ancestry, he was prohibited (as a rabbi had told him) from using phrases like "the God of our fathers" in reciting the liturgy, given that his fathers had not worshipped the God of Israel. This was on the face of it a halakhic question (one that, it may be recalled, was discussed by the early rabbis and that was being discussed in this same period by the important scholars known as the Tosafists in northern Europe; see chapter 3).[36] But its subtext was ontological, with psychological implications for the proselyte. Was a *ger* truly and entirely a Jew? Could a convert be recognized as such if he was differentiated from other Jews every time he prayed? Maimonides held that a *ger* could and should recite the liturgy like any other Jew. In explaining his reasoning, he expounded a conception according to which the *ger* became a Jew by virtue of being a student. (It may be recalled that the early rabbis had also represented the convert as a student.) Maimonides likened him to the members of Avraham's household (meaning his entire entourage) who, like his offspring, were first initiated into foundational theological truths before being taught "the ways of the Lord":

> Abraham our Father taught the entire people, enlightened them, and revealed to them the true faith [*da'at ha-emet*] and [the reality of] God's

> unity. He rejected idolatry and abolished its practices, and he gathered many under the wings of the Divine Presence. He provided them with instruction and guidance. He charged his descendants and subsequent "members of his household" with keeping the ways of the Lord forever, as Scripture states [Gen. 18:19], "For I have chosen him [Avraham], that he may instruct his children and his household after him to keep the way of the Lord."[37]

The exceptional respect with which Maimonides addressed Ovadiah ("our teacher and master Ovadiah, the wise and discerning proselyte"), and the firmness with which he denounced a rabbi who had called him a fool when Ovadiah had (rightly) argued that Islam was not idolatrous, give this letter an emotional force that is unusual in Maimonides' writings. Moshe Halbertal has commented that by rhetorically elevating Ovadiah and disparaging the rabbi in question, Maimonides "reversed the authority vector" between the rabbi and the convert. In any case, by emphasizing Ovadiah's intellectual and spiritual attainments he underscored a position that equalized the status of *ger* with that of Jews by ancestry.[38]

It was not in the letter to Ovadiah but in the *Mishneh Torah* that Maimonides laid out his definitive position on *giyyur*, one that was to become authoritative throughout the Jewish diaspora after its incorporation, in the sixteenth century, into the code of law known as the *Shulkhan Arukh*.[39] A key feature of the procedure he prescribed was the examination of the potential convert's motivations. Only if the candidate for *giyyur* had no ulterior motive—for example, the intention of marrying a Jew--and only if he or she was willing to accept "the heavy weight of the yoke of the Torah" was *giyyur* to proceed.[40] Put simply, religious motivation was the only acceptable motivation for conversion.[41] Once accepted, the *ger* was subject to certain halakhic restrictions but in essence was fully a Jew.

It would be a glaring omission not to mention the quite different conception of *giyyur* adopted by another influential Jewish thinker in the Islamic world. In contrast to Maimonides, the poet and philosopher Yehudah Halevi was troubled, as other Jews had been and would be, by the anomaly of the practice of *giyyur*, given the clarity with which Scripture differentiated between the Israelites—the descendants of Abraham, Isaac, and Jacob—and other nations. In his work the *Kuzari* (mentioned earlier in the discussion of the Khazars), Halevi writes, "Any Gentile who joins us unconditionally will enjoy our good fortune without, however, being quite equal to us."[42] Gentiles could gain merit by accepting the yoke of the Torah—they could become "pious and learned"—but they were incapable of reaching the highest level of spiritual achievement, namely prophecy.[43] Although Halevi's work the *Kuzari* had no practical implications for the practice of *giyyur*, it offered an alternative vision that would be developed along new lines in kabbalistic literature.

Apostasy

Whatever special qualities of soul that Jews may have been believed to possess, some Jews did choose to leave the Jewish community and join another religion. To be sure, despite the attractions of the majority society most Jews remained anchored in their communities, bound by a dense web of affective attachments. Yet Jewish apostasy was a fact of life, one that constituted an all-too-evident challenge to a radical essentialist conception of the Jew.

A thirteenth-century Jewish scholar wrote that "we never see anyone convert to Islam unless in terror, or in quest of power, or to avoid heavy taxation, or to escape humiliation, or if taken prisoner, or because of infatuation with a Muslim woman, or for some similar reason."[44] This statement is admittedly from a less than impartial source. Although Jews under Islam did suffer from stigma, legal disabilities, social discrimination, and occasional persecutions—and these were powerful reasons for apostasy—the wish to escape disabilities was not the only reason for joining the dominant religion. The author omitted more intangible motivations, such as the attraction of Islamic high culture or the sheer persuasiveness of Islamic triumph, which could sway the hesitant.[45] For Jews schooled in the unity of God, Islam's radical monotheism was among the factors that facilitated apostasy. Unlike the populations of other great powers under which Jews had lived from biblical times (including Christianity), Muslims were zealous in their worship of one indivisible God. This challenged in a fundamental way the Jews' ancient perception that they stood proudly alone in a world of idolatry. From a religious and psychic perspective, Islamic monotheism provided a bridge between two otherwise incompatible orthodoxies; crossing the threshold (at least in theory either way) was thus significantly eased.

We have documentation of Jewish apostasy primarily because of the legal issues raised when a Jew converted to Islam, which usually involved divorce, levirate marriage, inheritance, or lending on interest. These cases were complex because the apostate, while retaining the halakhic status of a Jew, did not automatically enjoy all the prerogatives of a Jew.[46] They were also complex because among the apostates to Islam were men and women whose trajectories challenge common understandings of the term "apostasy." In theory, the medieval milieu was a totalizing one in which the ritual act of conversion could not be a half- measure: Entry into one all-embracing field of existence meant absolute exit from another. Yet some Jewish apostates to Islam appear to have maintained significant attachments to the Jewish community. It was not uncommon, for example, for male apostates to remain married to unconverted Jewish women. Couples of this kind (and their children) often retained social and economic ties with Jewish communities.[47] It should be added that a Jewish woman who converted to Islam, unlike a man, was required under Islamic law to leave her Jewish spouse.

Rabbinic rulings about the status of apostates reflected both the perceived need to exclude from the community those who systematically violated halakha, on the one hand, and the wish to facilitate the sincere return to the Jewish community of such persons (and their children), on the other. Jews faced with disciplinary measures by communal leaders sometimes threatened to apostatize, a form of leverage that was used in later periods as well.[48] Apostasy did not necessarily, however, entail a radical severing of ties with Jewish society. Moshe Yagur writes that "a close examination of contacts between Jewish apostates and their former coreligionists in Geniza society reveals that, while apostasy was perceived negatively by Jewish community members, there are no signs of the excommunication of apostates, harassment of their families, considering the apostate as dead, or other social phenomena known from other periods and places in Jewish history."[49] Quotidian acceptance of rabbinically questionable social arrangements was apparently widespread.

The responsa dealing with cases of apostasy reveal little about the individuals involved, but other sources sometimes tell us more, especially when the converted Jews were of high status and possessed special polemical value to Muslim society.[50] A case in point is Yūsuf b. Ishāq b. Yahyā, a prominent Jewish judge (*dayyan*) who converted to Islam in Damascus in 1302. Yūsuf b. Yahyā's conversion (along with that of members of his family) was quite a public spectacle, with Islamic scholars and jurists in attendance. It was clearly organized to give the event maximum publicity. One account relates that "the viceroy [of Damascus] granted them [the converts] robes of honor and ordered that horses be prepared so they could ride in a parade in the city of Damascus and for drums to be beaten and horns to be played at the tail of the procession." One can well imagine the reaction to this display in the Jewish community.[51]

Apostates who openly polemicized against Judaism gained special notoriety among both Muslims and Jews. An early such case is that of Ya'qub ibn Killis (930–991). Born in Baghdad, Ibn Killis left Iraq for North Africa, where he became one of the principal architects of the ruling Fatimids' financial administration and eventually rose to power as vizier. He reportedly also became a respected scholar of Islamic law. As a vizier, a learned Muslim, and an apostate from Judaism, he was a walking polemical statement, and indeed he appears in two sources in an actively polemicizing stance. According to a Muslim account, Ibn Killis on one occasion attacked Judaism at a weekly gathering of intellectuals he convened, where Jews were present. He pointed out the "defects and faults" in Jewish teachings and asserted the Muslim claim that, although the Jews would not admit it, the name of the prophet Muhammed appears in the Torah. A different source, a Geniza fragment by a Jewish author, lends support to this account. That author was present at one such weekly gathering when Ibn Killis used an Arabic translation of the *siddur* (prayer book) of the eminent rabbi and philosopher Saadyah Gaon to ridicule Jewish prayers and beliefs. The fragment, in which he chastised Ibn Killis for having "vilified, ridiculed, and scorned the entire [Jewish] nation," appears to contain the opening lines of a treatise that did not survive defending Judaism against Ibn Killis's attack.[52]

Several learned apostates to Islam produced anti-Jewish polemical tracts in which they used their knowledge of Jewish texts to support Muslim exegetical claims. Their capacity to do this undoubtedly brought them prestige in their Islamic milieu.[53] The best known among them was Samaw'al al-Magribi, a respected twelfth-century mathematician, physician, and scholar. His autobiography suggests that important factors in his conversion to Islam were his early attraction to Islamic literature and his strong identification with a vision of Islam as the culmination of history, eclipsing both Judaism and Christianity.[54] This vision was integral to the argumentation of his popular and influential anti-Jewish polemical tract *Ifḥām al-Yahud* (Silencing the Jews). Not a modest man, Samaw'al referred to this work as "an exquisite tract of disputation against the Jews, the like of which had never been produced in Islam."[55]

Jews who converted to Islam did sometimes return to the Jewish community. Theoretically this was prohibited by Muslim law, but it was possible to evade the authorities.[56] Sources indicate considerable rabbinic lenience toward voluntary apostates who chose to return. For the most part, they were merely required to express their penitence, without undergoing any ritual act. Their status in the Jewish community then reverted to what it had been before they apostatized.[57]

Forced Conversion

The phrase "forced conversion" in the medieval period is likely to elicit an image of Jews being dragged to the baptismal font, rather than one of Jews being compelled to recite the Muslim *shahada* (see the later discussion). This is partly due to a widely recognized Jewish liturgical tradition that commemorates forced conversion and martyrdom in Christian lands and has no counterpart for Muslim lands. Theoretically, forced conversion was prohibited in Islamic law and (in contrast to canon law) was not valid if performed.[58] In practice, Jews, as a protected *dhimmi* people, rarely faced efforts to convert them against their will, even if they sometimes endured quite harsh policies that precipitated conversion. The single major episode of conversion under physical duress occurred under the Almohads, North African Berbers who in the twelfth century subjugated the Maghreb and southern Spain.[59] The Almohad conquerors revoked the protected *dhimmi* status of Jews (as well as that of Christians) and carried out a conversion campaign that gave Jews the choice between conversion or death. The overwhelming majority of Jews subjected to this policy chose to undergo conversion rather than flee or die.[60] Perhaps the Jews' awareness of *taqiyya*, the theologically sanctioned Muslim practice of dissimulating religious belief under the threat of persecution, made it easier for Jews to superficially accept Islam.[61]

Conversion to Islam was remarkably simple. Islamic law stipulated no ritual comparable to Christian baptism or Jewish immersion/circumcision. The only requirement was the pronouncement of the *shahada*, a brief acknowledgment of a single God and Muhammed as his prophet.[62] A letter from Fustat in 1148, written by a refugee from the Magreb, is a rare document describing how mass conversion was carried out in his town of Sijilmasa, a trade entrepot at the edge of the Sahara. He wrote that the Almohad ruler Abd al-Mu'min, after entering Sijilmasa in 1140, gathered the Jews of the town and tried first to convert them by debate and persuasion. After seven months of religious disputations, they were given the choice of conversion or death. One hundred and fifty Jews were killed, and the others converted. Similar campaigns took place throughout the conquered Almohad lands, although certain regions were spared. The climate of religious zealotry was eventually tempered. By 1160, when Maimonides' family settled in Fez, forced conversions were no longer taking place, and the "converts" were expected to adhere to Islam only quite perfunctorily.[63]

At the time of the brutal conversions of the 1140s, however, the forced converts faced a traumatic situation. Their synagogues were destroyed, many of their coreligionists had been killed, and their communal leaders had converted. In his *Iggeret Ha-Shemad* (Epistle on Martyrdom), Maimonides dealt with an inquiry sent by a potential victim of Almohad violence, whose anxieties were no doubt shared by other Jews in his predicament.[64] The author of the inquiry had earlier asked a rabbi whether he should accept conversion so as not to be killed, given the obligation in some circumstances for a Jew to accept martyrdom. The rabbi, declaring Islam to be a form of idolatry, replied that whoever uttered the Muslim conversion formula was a Gentile, even if "he fulfills the entire Law publicly and privately."[65]

Maimonides, in his sharp response, sought to strip the coerced act of reciting the *shahada* of any religious significance or psychological power. Was it conceivable, he asked rhetorically, that God would not reward Jews who, despite being forced to go through a conversion ritual, performed commandments secretly? What the victims had done was merely to mouth some words; they had not been forced to take any actions. "In this persecution [the victims] are not required to do anything, but only to say something. . . . This compulsion imposes no action, only speech. . . . There has never been a persecution as remarkable as this one, where the only coercion is to say something."[66] Islam was not, in any case, an idolatrous religion, and even if it was, a Jew who committed idolatry did not thereby become a Gentile—as the Hebrew Bible demonstrated repeatedly. Maimonides' advice to the potential victim, under the circumstances, was to recite the required phrase and avoid death. His status would not be affected by his life-preserving act. Once he had converted to Islam, however, it would be incumbent on him to flee to freedom when possible.

Christendom

Voluntary Converts

Despite the wide diffusion of the church's hostile representations of Jews and Judaism in the medieval period, small numbers of Christians nevertheless chose to join the Jewish community. It is often from Geniza documents that we learn about such Christian converts, because many of them fled to Muslim lands to escape punishment for their apostasy. Yet quite a few converts remained in Christian lands, some apparently unmolested and perhaps escaping detection by changing residence. There were cases in which the Christian authorities were satisfied with a heavy fine for a Christian's conversion to Judaism.[67] In other cases, converts to Judaism returned to the church and were reconciled and absolved of their sin of apostasy.[68] But especially in the later medieval period, as the church became increasingly militant, punishment for a Christian who underwent *giyyur* could be violent, as in the 1222 case of a former deacon in England who was hanged for his betrayal.[69] It was not only the converts themselves who were endangered by the step they took: The church prohibited Jews from any involvement in the conversion of a Christian, and punishment by local authorities could be severe.[70] In 1278 a rabbi in Toulouse was burned by the Inquisition on a charge of proselytizing, and there were other such incidents.[71] Certainly, it is not always possible to ascertain whether charges of Jewish proselytizing were grounded in fact: They could be one of the many imagined forms of Jewish perfidy.[72]

Under the circumstances, the small number of converts is not surprising, even if the documentation is imperfect. Only about eighty cases have been identified for the period from the eleventh to fourteenth centuries.[73] But although the numbers are low, these conversions were heavily weighted with theological significance for both sides in a bitter polemical struggle. Their impact was magnified for the church because the outward conflict with Judaism was mirrored by an internal struggle, one that Bernard Blumenkranz has called a "fight to overcome the Jewish inheritance within the Church."[74] The problem, at heart, was the difficulty involved in reading the Old Testament as a Christian text. Doing so required interpreting critical passages in a way that could not but raise doubts and disagreements among educated Christians. The key doctrines of the trinity and incarnation were particularly difficult to reconcile with the simple sense of the text. It is thus no accident that so many medieval Christian converts to Judaism were clerics, nobles, or both and that some participated actively after their conversion in the very polemical struggle that they had grappled with personally in their path to conversion.[75]

What did Jews think about the rare cases of Christian *giyyur*? On the one hand, there is evidence that proselytes were sometimes disparaged, in time-honored fashion, because of their Gentile lineage or at least were regarded as having a status inferior to that of Jews by ancestry.[76] The fact that the community could be put at risk by accepting them also surely complicated their reception.[77] On the other hand, proselytes offered valuable affirmation for an embattled Jewry that it was the Jews who held the true interpretation of scripture. Northern French and German Tosafists often expressed admiration and support for converts.[78] Christians who underwent *giyyur* despite the risk of severe punishment or death enhanced the ethos of martyrdom that was integral to late medieval Jewish ideology in Christian Europe.[79] The Memorbuch of Mainz, in a list of Jews killed in Wissembourg in 1270 that included three proselytes, added, in a phrase laden with pathos, this detail about one proselyte: He was "the head of all those who go barefoot [i.e., Franciscans], who abhorred images and took shelter under the wings of the Eternal and was burned as a martyr."[80]

Although in some circles persecution may have enhanced the image of converts who were stalwart in defying Christian teaching, in others that same persecution may have reinforced a tendency to see the Gentile as an essentially alien being, incapable of full assimilation into the Jewish people. Such a perception, in any case, was vividly expressed in the *Zohar*, a seminal kabbalistic work composed in thirteenth-century Spain. Elaborating on the distinction between Gentile and Jew in a loose, unsystematic fashion within the symbolic conceptual universe of kabbalistic speculation, the *Zohar* situated the origins of the Gentile in the *Sitra ahra*, the demonic "other side," in contrast to the Jew, whose origins were in the divine "holy seed." Insincere converts remained fully within the domain of the *Sitra ahra* and posed a stumbling block to the Jews into whose midst they came. But what was the nature of sincere converts in this binary cosmos? According to one passage, the righteous convert was able to rescue sparks of holiness that, because of the extraordinary power of divine illumination, were diffused beyond the divine realm into the world of evil. Yet the *Sitra ahra* maintained a hold even on *gerei tzedek* because, unlike the Israelites, they were not of "purely holy seed." Their children, too, were tainted with impurity, and it was only in the third generation that they would be fully purged.[81]

Neither the legal nor the literary sources produced by Jews in medieval Christendom offer much insight into the lives of flesh-and-blood converts. From Christian sources we know of their existence mainly from the repeated prohibitions in church law of conversion to Judaism and from records of the papal Inquisition.[82] The converts about whose lives we are best informed are those who attracted public attention, usually by polemicizing against Christianity. The earliest case on record, known only through Latin sources, was that of a deacon named Bodo in the French court of Louis the Pious. The chronicler Prudentius describes Bodo as the scion of an important Frankish family who had received a "courtly education." In 838 he sought permission from the emperor to go to Rome. But once in Rome (or possibly after he left Rome), he converted to Judaism. The chronicler relates that "once circumcised, he let the hair of his head and beard grow long" and called himself Eliezer. He settled in Saragossa, Spain, which was then under Muslim rule. There he studied Torah and, in 840, engaged in a literary debate with a Jewish convert to Christianity living in Cordova. The debate revolved around the classic issues of Christian–Jewish polemics: whether Jesus was the messiah prophesied in Jewish Scripture, whether Christians were the true Israel, and whether Christianity was the fulfillment of the Old Testament. Unfortunately, Bodo's arguments were torn from the single existing manuscript record of the debate, presumably to prevent their dissemination.[83]

A case from the early eleventh century has similar features. A Latin chronicler reported that a former cleric at a ducal court named Wecelin, who had been "won over to the error of the Jews"—apparently in 1006 in one of the major Rhineland communities—was the author of a statement repudiating Christianity. The chronicler included in his account the short tract he ascribed to Wecelin. Citing Scripture, the author of the tract argued that incarnation was impossible because God's nature did not change and further that God's covenant with Israel could not be abrogated. These arguments may have been preserved thanks to the German monarch, who ordered the chronicler to add a refutation of them.[84]

A century later, in 1102, the conversion of another Ovadiah "the *Ger*," this one an educated Italian nobleman and priest originally named Johannes, reflected the same basic trajectory. A letter of recommendation written on his behalf years after his *giyyur* by a rabbi in Aleppo described him as "expert in the study of their [the Christians'] books," who "because he understood what he read in the books of their false doctrines" decided to turn to the God of Israel "and officially embraced Judaism before a Jewish court."[85] In an autobiographical account in Hebrew that he wrote at some time after 1121, Ovadiah related that when he was a child in southern Italy the conversion to Judaism in Constantinople of the archbishop of Bari, Andreas, made a strong impression on him.[86] He was moved to take the step of conversion himself by the enduring memory of an apocalyptic dream in his youth, one that featured a darkly prophetic verse from the book of Joel. His conversion to Judaism was initially a "self-conversion" that he undertook while still living in a Christian community. He performed circumcision on himself (as he reported Andreas had also done), after which he observed "the holidays of God, as they are written in the Torah," as well as the Sabbath. A Geniza fragment relates Ovadiah's subsequent experiences in Bagdad, where the head of the academy, Isaac ben Moses, instructed him, together with orphaned children, in the Hebrew Bible.[87]

The timing of Ovadiah's conversion and his preoccupation with the verse in question (Joel 2:31 of the Vulgate) have led to speculation that he was swayed to take this radical step by Christian eschatological expectations that were widespread around the time of the First Crusade, an episode of which he was keenly aware.[88] Apocalyptic currents may help explain the audacious and even reckless behavior of other such converts. One educated eleventh-century convert, for example, related in a letter written in awkward Hebrew that, as a monk or cleric, he had circumcised himself and begun to observe Jewish precepts. But driven by zeal, he had given an "important priest" fourteen polemical treatises against Christianity and asked to have them read publicly, confident that they would bring other Christians to convert. He was imprisoned but escaped with the help of a guard.[89]

Similarly, in 1254 a Christian convert to Judaism from Augsburg provoked his former coreligionists by desecrating crucifixes or images of saints; he was tortured and burned at the stake. A *payyetan* (liturgical poet) who commemorated the episode wrote that this convert, who "yearned to present himself as a burnt offering," entered a church and, shattering an idol, demanded, "Where is their god [Deut. 32:37]?"[90] Such demonstrative, public actions recall the behavior of Jews by ancestry whose impassioned acts of resistance to forced conversion in the late medieval period were glorified in martyrological accounts.[91]

Far from the high drama of such feverish acts were cases of an entirely different kind. In Christian Europe as in Islam, partial *giyyur* was required by halakha for slaves in a Jewish household. Even though the church disapproved of Jews holding dominion over non-Jews and Jews were thus not, theoretically, allowed to own slaves, some Jews in Christian Europe did have slaves, although far less commonly than under Islam. It particularly scandalized the church that some of these slaves were baptized Christians.[92] Pope Gregory IX complained about the practice of German Jews circumcising slaves in a letter to German prelates in 1233.[93] As was the case under Islam, slaves owned by Jews were frequently freed; this is evident from the various formulas for certificates of manumission—*shtarei shikhrur*—provided by halakhists. In effect such certificates, as discussed earlier, recognized a freed slave as a full member of the Jewish community. Although the evidence of actual cases is scarce, such integration seems to have occurred.[94] Yet this was not the only way that slaves owned by Jews could be emancipated. By law, pagan or Muslim slaves held by a Jew could gain their freedom by declaring their intention to be baptized—a practice the church encouraged by compensating the Jewish owner for the financial loss.[95]

Voluntary Apostasy

As with Jews under Islam, the attractions of apostasy for Jews in Christendom were varied and defy easy generalization. Personal predicaments could be the catalyst for escape through conversion. The disabilities suffered by Jews as a minority provided an impetus to undergo baptism. Jews could also evade prosecution for a crime by accepting baptism, and accused offenders often availed themselves of this apparently painless path to freedom. But some were no doubt swayed by the church's increasingly sophisticated conversionist offensive, of a kind unknown under Islam.

From a Christian perspective, the Jews' continued adherence to the "Old Law"—the "dead" law in Christian theology—posed an implicit challenge to basic Christian claims. It is what prompted the church fathers and the theologians who succeeded them to produce a voluminous anti-Jewish polemical literature. Yet for centuries these texts were intended only for Christian consumption. It was not until the thirteenth century that the church (and frequently monarchs as well) initiated an aggressive missionizing campaign directed at Jews, one that was novel both in its argumentation (including a concerted attack on the Talmud) and in its practical implementation (including forced sermons and the staging of religious disputations).[96] Although this campaign caused no little distress to Jewish communities, it did not necessarily produce converts in significant numbers.[97]

Jews who chose baptism by no means chose an easy life. They were often regarded with suspicion by other Christians. Moreover, because they forfeited their property on conversion, they were frequently destitute. Begging licenses were issued to some of them. Many became, as it were, professional converts, wandering from town to town begging for alms, with licenses describing their conversion in idealized, formulaic terms that undoubtedly often hid a more sordid reality. In England a Domus Conversorum (Home for Converts) was established in 1232 to provide shelter and a stipend to converts, but even its residents were sometimes forced to resort to begging.[98]

Studies in both medieval Aragon and early modern Germany indicate that it was less frequent for women than for men to apostatize independently of a spouse. (When women did so, it was often to escape an abusive husband or one who refused to grant them a *get*.[99]) Men may have had greater opportunities to engage with the non-Jewish world, stirring aspirations for career opportunities that were not open to them as Jews. When they apostatized, their wives were likely to follow them, because such women ran great risks if they refused to do so. If their apostate husbands would not give them a *get*, they would be unable to remarry. Moreover, their husbands could gain custody of their children according to canon law. And if apostate husbands later returned to the Jewish community, their Jewish wives might be held guilty of luring them back or even of the crime of engaging in sexual relations with a baptized Christian.[100]

As with Christian converts to Judaism, a good deal more is known about baptized Jewish intellectuals than about less educated apostates. Educated converts sometimes rose to considerable prominence in the Christian world as adversaries of Judaism. Like educated Jews who converted to Islam, their knowledge placed them in a strategic position to polemicize for their new faith. They argued, like converts to Islam, that the Jews had misinterpreted or falsified the revealed text of the Torah and that their newly adopted faith superseded Judaism. Yet for reasons that had to do with the specific Christian need to discredit Judaism and bring Jews to conversion, Jewish apostates who polemicized against Judaism attained a singular place in the public arena. The best known among them—Nicholas Donin, Pablo Christiani, Alfonso de Valladolid, Pablo de Santa Maria, and Jerónimo de Santa Fe—inflicted considerable damage on the Jewish community through their polemicizing. Especially injurious were staged public disputations at which Jews were constrained from making effective counterarguments.[101] The situational triggers that brought these men to baptism differed greatly, but for all of them, being a Christian with a Jewish past was closely bound up with the task of disavowing and refuting Judaism.[102] As one scholar has noted, the conversion narratives of such apostates were themselves "a form of religious apologetic."[103]

In the highly charged atmosphere of the late medieval Christian orbit, Jews were known to hurl insults at apostates, and as a general rule the latter were not mourned when they died.[104] Yet even though for the most part apostates lived outside the well-defined boundaries of the Jewish community and were considered a disgrace, there is evidence that in the small towns of Ashkenaz, the northern European Jewish orbit, they sometimes interacted in routine ways with their ex-coreligionists.[105]

There was considerable variation in the rulings of Ashkenazi halakhists in cases that involved apostates. It was a foundational principle established by Rashi in the eleventh century that a Jew, "even if he sinned" (that is, by being baptized), remained a Jew.[106] Yet subsequent rabbinic scholars debated whether this was entirely so. Was the meat of animals slaughtered by an apostate kosher? Were the children of a (female) apostate Jews? Could an apostate inherit from other Jews? Could a Jew lend money on interest to an apostate? On such issues halakhists sometimes ruled that apostates were to be treated as if they were non-Jews. However, in the areas of marriage and divorce the apostate remained a Jew, even though the consequences were sometimes painful—as when a woman could not obtain a *get* from her apostate husband or when a childless widow's apostate brother-in-law refused to perform the ritual required for her remarriage.[107]

Many apostates, it appears, became disillusioned in one way or another with their lives in the Christian orbit and sought to return to the Jewish community. The Tosafist Isaac ben Samuel went so far as to claim that most apostates "regret their actions immediately but are afraid of the non-Jews, and so they go to a different place and return there."[108] Especially in the late medieval period, the punishments meted out by the church when a baptized Jew returned to the Jewish community could be quite draconian and might include death.[109] Yet many apostates did return, relocating themselves or otherwise staying beneath the Christian authorities' radar.

Although from a formal halakhic point of view returning apostates had never ceased to be Jews, and although it was forbidden to remind them of their prior status, the intuitive popular view held that a ritual was needed to mark their reentry into the community. It became the norm for the returning apostate to undergo immersion to "nullify" baptism and to purify the penitent of idolatrous contamination. From the late twelfth century onward, a number of halakhists provided legal justification for this custom, even if it was not obligatory.[110] The fourteenth-century French inquisitor Bernard Gui, who gathered detailed testimony from accused relapsed converts to Christianity, reported that when such immersions took place the benediction for immersion was uttered not before but after immersion.[111] This is a revealing detail and aligns with the ruling of R. Eliezer ben Yoel ha-Levi, who noted that the immersing returnee was "like a *ger*" who could not make the benediction before formally becoming a Jew.[112] At least symbolically, immersion "rejudaized" the apostate.

Immersion alone, however, was not always deemed sufficient to mark the transition. It was only one of the elements of the ritual that Bernard Gui described. Before immersion, he wrote, the returnees were rubbed vigorously with sand, especially in the places where, during baptism, they were anointed with consecrated oil. In addition, the nails of the hands and feet were cut until they bled, and the head was shaved. There were symbolic, purifying aspects to this ritual, but the corrosive rubbing and cutting of the flesh suggest a penitential aspect as well.[113] Other sources also prescribed penitential acts in addition to immersion. The thirteenth-century German Pietist R. Eleazar of Worms, in his penitential treatises, prescribed rigorous penances for the returning apostate, including fasting, abstaining from meat or wine, and refraining from bathing.[114] Such practices were not, however, uniquely reserved for returning apostates: Penitential practices were widespread in Ashkenazi communities and were prescribed for a wide range of sins. They thus did not mark the returning apostate as categorically distinct from other offending Jews.

The grimness with which late medieval Jews viewed the act of apostasy in the emotionally charged environment they inhabited is reflected in a confession made to the Inquisition by Jews in Aragon in 1341. Two witnesses confessed to having instructed a deeply repentant apostate (who corroborated their testimony) to display his contrition by an act that courted martyrdom: He was to demand from Christian officials that they amputate those fingers with which he had made the sign of the cross, rip off the skin of the forehead that had come into contact with chrism (the oil used to anoint a person undergoing baptism), and flay the skin of his knees on which he had knelt before crucifixes. This provocative and unhinged demand, which had been made of another repentant apostate seven years earlier, suggests just how emotionally difficult it might be to accept the apostate back and how literally the term *meshumad* might be taken.[115]

Forced Conversion

At several junctures in the medieval period, Jews submitted to baptism under threat of death during waves of anti-Jewish violence. These Jews experienced "conversion" in a particular way, as a sudden and profoundly traumatic act forced on them.[116] Two major episodes are standard features of Jewish historiography: the First Crusade in the Rhineland in 1096 (mentioned earlier), and the riots in Spain in 1391. The long-term effects of the former were mainly spiritual and emotional, shaping Ashkenazi consciousness for centuries; the latter had more concrete consequences, creating an enduring population of unwilling converts of an unprecedented size and importance.[117]

Jewish scholars once drew a sharp contrast between these two episodes. They counterposed the purported readiness for martyrdom of Ashkenazic Jews, when faced with the choice of baptism or death, with the purported readiness of Sephardic Jews to accept baptism in the same situation. Today it is evident that no such clear-cut difference existed. During both episodes, many of the Jews who were killed were never given the choice to save themselves by conversion but were simply slaughtered. Of those who were offered the alternative of conversion, some chose conversion, but others (in *both* episodes) chose a martyr's death. In the charged religious atmosphere of the attacks, accepting baptism could be envisioned by both Ashkenazi and Spanish Jews as not only a breach of faith but also an abhorrent—even unthinkable—act.[118]

In the wake of the First Crusade violence of 1096, the emperor granted permission for the victims to return to the Jewish community, apparently with the acquiescence of the pope.[119] Their return to the Jewish community a short time after they had been forcibly baptized surely minimized the trauma and psychic dislocation involved. A quick return also eased the converts' reacceptance by the Jewish community. Nevertheless, in a responsum in the wake of the First Crusade Rashi prohibited the shaming of returnees, suggesting that such incidents did occur.[120]

Over the course of the twelfth century, church policy changed. Although technically the forcible baptism of a Jew was still prohibited (this had always been church teaching), even a forcibly baptized Jew was now forbidden from reverting to Judaism: In 1201 a new papal definition of "compulsion" in effect rendered even violently performed baptisms "voluntary."[121] Of course, even unforced baptisms did not fully merit the definition of "voluntary." Inflammatory anti-Jewish preaching (including sermons forced on Jewish congregations), economic restrictions and special taxes, quotidian humiliations like having to wear the Jewish badge, and the threat of expulsion were among factors that pressured Jews to convert.

Conversion did not, however, necessarily provide conditions for a better life, and baptized Jews frequently regretted their decision. Yet returning to

Jewish life was not always an option. Doing so became increasingly dangerous after the church, in its campaign against heresy, established the papal Inquisition in the thirteenth century. Although initially the primary targets of inquisitorial prosecutions were sincere Christians with heterodox ideas, baptized "judaizers" were also classified as heretics and were potentially subject to death at the stake. The papal bull *Turbato corde*, when reissued in 1274, singled out for punishment "*rejudaizantes*," as well as Jews who facilitated the latter's return. In southern France and Italy where the papal Inquisition was active, punishment for aiding the return of a baptized Jew was in some instances imposed on an entire Jewish community.[122] With its coercive methods, the Inquisition was able to gather detailed information about those involved. It is telling that some inquisitors were even familiar with the rabbinic term that Jews used to refer to the "rejudaized" convert, namely "*ba'al teshuvah*," or one who transgresses and repents.[123]

The forcible baptisms of Jews in late fourteenth-century Spain were unique in their scope and long-term impact. They took place during anti-Jewish riots that swept through Castile and Aragon, devastating dozens of Jewish communities and leaving some without even a single unbaptized member.[124] It was by this time well established that a convert's return to Judaism after baptism, regardless of the circumstances of the conversion, was a crime punishable by death. In effect, a new kind of population was created, comprising persons known in Hebrew as *anusim* ("forced ones") and in Spanish as *conversos* ("converts") or *nuevos cristianos* (New Christians). Perversely—and with unanticipated consequences—descendants of the original converts continued for generations to be known as "conversos" or "New Christians" and suffered from discrimination. To be sure, some lived a crypto-Jewish existence, but others rather quickly assimilated to Spanish Catholic life.

The 1391 riots in Spain set in motion forces that would dominate Iberian Jewish history for the following three centuries and longer, raising issues that are integral to this book. However, these developments more properly belong to the early modern period, which saw in Jewish society, as well as in Reformation-age Europe in general, the erosion of relatively stable medieval structures and the emergence, after a period of turmoil, of dominant new structures.

Conclusion

It is no mystery why, in the medieval period, few Gentiles chose to become Jews. Despite the diverse conditions of life across an expansive Jewish diaspora, Jews everywhere lived under either Christian or Muslim rule and were subject to restrictions, special taxes, and popular hostility. In both orbits, converting to Judaism was prohibited and could be punished with death. Yet in addition to the few brave and spiritually driven *gerim* in this period, a significant number of converts entered the Jewish community by a less-than-voluntary path. These were emancipated slaves, mainly in Islamic lands, who underwent a partial form of conversion when they were initially purchased by Jews and became full members of the Jewish community on their manumission.

The same conditions that inhibited Gentiles from choosing to become Jews in this period encouraged Jews to convert "out" and join the dominant religion. From the thirteenth century onward, the church's missionizing played a role. It has often been assumed that, given the exclusivism of the medieval church and to a lesser extent Islam, apostasy meant severing all ties to Jewish life. This was not always the case, however, and some apostates eventually returned to the Jewish community.

5 Early Modern

In the medieval period, religious boundary crossing between Jewish and Gentile communities followed a few basic pathways. The passage was marked by a ritual act supervised by religious authorities, one that clearly marked the adoption of a new (or renewed) socioreligious identity. Although this remained the conceptual norm, the breakdown (or partial breakdown) of medieval religious structures in early modern Europe (mid-fifteenth to the mid-eighteenth centuries) led to the emergence of new pathways and patterns of "conversion." The radical alteration of the religious landscape of Reformation Europe is key to any discussion of Jews and conversion in this period. The breakup of a monolithic western Catholic Church and the emergence of diverse forms of Protestant Christianity, the religious wars that ensued, the accommodation of some societies to a multireligious environment, and concerted efforts by others to suppress heterodoxy—all these had consequences for the ways in which conversion to and from Judaism took place.

As in the medieval period, the best-documented converts to Judaism in Reformation Europe were highly educated men driven by doubts about basic Christian doctrines. Yet they often differed from their medieval predecessors. Their thinking tended to reflect a new sensibility, with elements of anticlericalism, tolerationism, and skeptical thinking. Perhaps surprisingly, sensibilities of this kind could be found not only in Protestant Europe but also in the deeply repressive societies of Catholic Spain and Portugal—primarily among conversos but even among "Old Christians" with no Jewish ancestry, some of whom underwent dramatic spiritual conversions to "the Law of Moses." To be sure, formal conversion to Judaism was not an option in the Iberian orbit. Yet heterodox currents flowed beneath the surface, and crypto-Jews who cultivated "judaizing" traditions presented a relatively robust (if dangerous) alternative to Catholic orthodoxy.

The same theological upheaval that led to new patterns of conversion to Judaism also led to new patterns of voluntary Jewish apostasy. There were always Jews who converted to the dominant religion to escape difficult personal predicaments. This period, however, saw conversions of a novel and subversive nature, as believers in the messiahship of Sabbatai Zevi underwent formal conversions to Islam and (under pressure) to Christianity. Even though the Dönmeh in the Ottoman Empire and the Frankists in Poland were quite different, members of both groups understood their conversions in mythic, kabbalistic terms as a necessary element in their heretical but distinctly Jewish beliefs.

Except for studies on the Sabbatean episode and the Dönmeh, scholarship about issues of conversion under Islam in this period is meager, in part due to the scarcity of sources. For Iran, a study of two episodes of forced or fear-driven Jewish apostasy in the seventeenth and eighteenth centuries, based mainly on Judeo-Persian accounts, stands alone.[1] A study of Jewish slave ownership in the Ottoman Empire discusses the integration into Jewish life of freed slaves (mostly female) owned by Jews.[2] And an article on *shariah* court records of conversions to Islam in the Ottoman Empire reveals some of the personal, situational strategies behind the conversions of Jewish women to Islam.[3] Ottoman court records from early modern Jerusalem dealing with Jewish conversion to Islam have been translated to Hebrew and published, and Amnon Cohen, the primary scholar on this topic, has briefly discussed them elsewhere.[4] These studies together seem to confirm an Islamic approach to conversion that was less fraught and dogmatic than the Christian approach to baptism, but in the absence of a fuller picture this chapter focuses on developments in the Christian world.[5]

The Northern Reformation

In the popular imagination the Reformation began on October 31, 1517, when an Augustinian monk named Martin Luther issued his Ninety-Five Theses against indulgences, purportedly nailing them to the door of the Castle Church in Wittenberg. Scholars, not satisfied with such convenient dramatizations, have long seen the origins of the Reformation in calls for reform within the Catholic Church that dated back to the fourteenth century. Italian humanism was instrumental in shaping a new sensibility: However simplistic, there is some truth to the aphorism that Erasmus laid the egg that Luther hatched. What distinguished Luther's defiance of papal authority was the princely support he received, which allowed him to set in motion the processes that reconfigured European life over the next two centuries. Luther's "self-conversion" became an inspiration for a wider popular wave of conversion to Protestant beliefs and practices, one that was not seen to require re-baptism or any other ritual. Luther's success in sparking a widespread rejection of papal authority and establishing a conception of religious authority that was lodged in Scripture opened the way for a cascade of later innovations. The transformation was greatly facilitated by Luther's encouragement of independent lay Bible reading, which became an integral aspect of Protestant culture.

Luther famously expected that with the reformation of Christianity the Jews, whom he viewed as having been justifiably repelled by the abuses of the Catholic Church (among them a corrupt papacy and priesthood), would flock to the baptismal font. His later vitriolic anti-Jewish writings are widely understood to reflect, among other things, his disappointment that Jews did not fulfill his hopes. However, the Protestant movement continued to missionize, and individual Jews continued to apostatize. It is unfortunate that the rich autobiographical record left by baptized German Jews in the early modern period offers little insight into the authors' inner lives. Their narratives are shaped to fit the expectations of their new environment, and they denigrate Jews and Judaism in a flat and formulaic style.[6] Converts who met with disappointment in their new lives sometimes returned to the Jewish community, despite the risks involved. One eighteenth-century baptized German Jew described an elaborate rite he was required to undergo to be received back into the community, including immersion before a *beit din*.[7]

As in the medieval period, learned apostates in Reformation Germany played an important role in the production of anti-Jewish propaganda. Just before Luther appeared on the scene, Johannes Pfefferkorn, the Dominican apostate from Judaism, launched a wholesale attack on Jewish texts as slanderous to Christianity. Famously, the Christian Hebraist Johann Reuchlin, increasingly at odds with the Dominicans, refuted that blanket accusation—citing in support of his position another Jewish apostate, the learned fifteenth-century Spanish author Paul of Burgos (Pablo de Santa Maria) whose widely disseminated *Scrutinium scripturarum* offered support to Reuchlin's insistence on the polemical value of rabbinic texts.[8]

But the terms of discourse were changing. Although sixteenth-century Protestants saw their primary theological enemy as not the Jews but the Catholic Church, they envisioned Catholics and Jews as sharing negative characteristics. Among the various accusations leveled at the Catholic Church was its abandonment of apostolic simplicity and its production of fabricated ceremonies. Protestants could see Catholicism as having in this way "judaized" Christian worship, producing what they viewed as a plethora of invented rituals and ceremonies just as the Jews did. Accordingly, some learned apostates in Reformation-age Germany—most notably the rabbi-turned-priest Victor von Carben and the son and grandson of rabbis Anthonius Margaritha—focused not on polemical arguments about scriptural interpretation, as learned medieval Jewish apostates had done, but on the labyrinthine world of Jewish custom, with its supposed sordid, anti-Christian "secrets."[9]

Alongside this development and in tension with it, Christian Hebraists were exploring Jewish texts with the aim of enriching a Christian tradition whose textual roots were Jewish. They too took an interest in the world of Jewish ritual. The many works on Jewish custom produced by Christian Hebraists in this period, among them Johannes Buxtorf's massive *Synagoga Judaica* (1603), made the intimate everyday experience of Jewish life newly accessible to Christians. Although the Hebraists' work was not without bias, it reflected a scholarly discipline and concern for accuracy that were lacking in the propagandistic works of converts from Judaism like Carben and Margaritha. To carry out their work they needed Jews or Jewish converts to teach them Hebrew and to aid them in the work of printing Hebrew books. Jews and former Jews also served as their ethnographic informants, reporting on customs and practices that Christian Hebraists knew only from books, if at all.[10] Although the advantages of apostasy for Jews in the book industry could be substantial, they could also come at a high price.[11] Still, Christian Hebraism opened up respectable professional opportunities for baptized Jews who might otherwise have lived at the margins of the Christian community or desisted from conversion altogether.

Paradoxically, the same environment of humanist scholarship and print culture that nurtured Jewish apostasy gave rise to remarkable new instances of Christian conversion to Judaism.[12] Several factors were at work. A more open-minded curiosity about the way Jews lived developed as part of an increasing openness to foreign mores, as European expansion stimulated interest in exotic human customs. At least among Christian nonconformists and religious seekers, a more inquisitive sensibility led to genuine consideration of radical alternatives to traditions that seemed an accident of birth. In addition, the bewildering fragmentation of a Christian world that had been united for centuries prompted a search for firm spiritual ground. Catholics, Lutherans, Calvinists, Zwinglians, and Anabaptists, not to mention Anti-Trinitarians—Who was to say which was the one true faith? The discord between Christian confessions raised the possibility that none reflected God's will. The religious wars of the sixteenth and seventeenth centuries underscored the problem. Bitter divisions arose even within confessions, as demonstrated by the violent conflict among Calvinists in the Netherlands. Johan Peter Späth was not alone when, in the 1680s, he asked "whether there might not be a touchstone or sign by which . . . one could know who has the correct truth and knowledge since so many all over the world differ from each other."[13]

Späth eventually answered his question when in 1696, after a long spiritual odyssey, he converted to Judaism in Amsterdam. Part of the appeal of Judaism, which he understood in complex and idiosyncratic terms, was the fact that the rabbinic tradition had preserved its unity over the centuries. Such a tradition could be seen as harboring a primordial kernel of truth, and Späth found in it a refuge of certainty. The young Frenchman Aaron d'Antan, also a complex figure, followed a somewhat similar path when he underwent *giyyur* in Amsterdam around 1701.[14] For these two men Judaism was attractive for its perceived fixity in a world of spiritual flux and instability.

Although it was no accident that both Späth and d'Antan converted in the city of Amsterdam, it should be noted that they did so at the turn of the eighteenth century. In the seventeenth century the Dutch Republic, despite its reputation for tolerance, drew the line when it came to converting Gentiles to Judaism. Amsterdam regulations of 1616 prohibited the conversion and circumcision of Gentiles (though they did not prevent occasional cases of *giyyur*).[15] Ex-conversos who "returned" to Judaism were another matter and are discussed later; their Jewish ancestry and history of persecution under Catholic rule made their turn to Judaism acceptable to the Dutch authorities.

The structures of power were quite different in lands where the Catholic Church was struggling to regain its supremacy in the wake of the Reformation. Especially in Italy and in the separate case of Iberia (discussed in greater detail later), the effort to impose Catholic orthodoxy on all subjects of the realm assumed unprecedented thoroughness. The church's aggressive missionizing efforts were naturally directed at Jews (or judeo-conversos), but they were also aimed at heterodox Catholics (and, in Spain, *moriscos*, the descendants of forcibly baptized Muslims).

In sixteenth- and seventeenth-century Italy, the Catholic Church's measures to exert pressure on Jews to convert, either directly or indirectly, were not notable for their subtlety. Among them were ghettoization, the censorship of Hebrew books, and compulsory attendance at conversionary sermons. Occasionally the benefits of converting were hard to resist: Among other incentives, baptism offered condemned Jewish criminals a reprieve from punishment.[16] Houses of catechumens were established to instruct and otherwise support the conversion of neophytes.[17] As earlier in the Renaissance period, a few converts were able to parlay their Jewish knowledge into careers; however, by the sixteenth century they did so not as learned Hebraists but as participants in a religiously repressive regime, censoring Hebrew books and polemicizing against Judaism.[18]

In Poland-Lithuania, which had been a breeding ground for heterodox thought in the early Reformation period, the Catholic Church reasserted its authority and launched a missionizing program in the late seventeenth century. Up to that point, Jewish apostasy had been rare. It is true that during the violence of the Chmielnitsky massacres of 1648 Jews were forcibly baptized. But Polish King Jan Kazimierz quickly decreed that they could return "to their former faith," and according to the Jewish chronicler Nathan Hanover they did so freely.[19] Concerted Jesuit missionizing efforts a few decades later—directed at Calvinists and Lutherans, as well as Jews—do not appear from the documentation to have yielded impressive results.[20]

The Iberian Case

The circumstances that led to the rupture of old religious identities in post-expulsion Spain and early modern Portugal defied traditional patterns of conversion so starkly that they deserve a separate discussion. As mentioned in the previous section, a population of forced Jewish converts—known as "conversos" or "New Christians"—was created in Spain during widespread anti-Jewish riots in 1391. In the century that followed, they and their descendants either assimilated to Catholic life or learned to accommodate outwardly to Catholicism while maintaining a clandestine Jewish existence.[21] Yet they all remained "conversos" or "New Christians," terms that came to signify their Jewish ancestry. Those who secretly adhered to Jewish beliefs and practices were heretics in the eyes of the church; if suspected of "judaizing," they could be tried by bishops and, theoretically, put to death. Unbaptized Jews were also at risk for prosecution if they offered support to judaizers—for example, by supplying them with kosher meat or teaching them Jewish prayers. Under such conditions, the usual lines drawn between apostates and normative Jews—and the moral judgments they implied—were profoundly blurred.

Reports of converso judaizing were the catalyst that led to the establishment of the Spanish Inquisition in 1478. Indeed, the Inquisition exposed the extent to which unbaptized Jews were aiding judaizers. This evidence provided the explicit rationale for expelling the Jews from Spain in 1492—a step that spelled the end of normative Jewish life on Spanish soil. Yet secret converso judaizing persisted long after the expulsion, as the vast corpus of Inquisition trial records shows. For generations, in the absence of Jewish texts and institutions, judaizers relied on oral traditions to transmit such fundamental Jewish teachings as the unity of God and the obligation to observe the "Law of Moses." In the course of time those traditions became increasingly impoverished and detached from their roots in medieval Iberian rabbinic Judaism.

In 1497 the Portuguese crown, under pressure from the Spanish monarchs, ordered its own Jews (including many exiles from Spain) forcibly converted en masse, creating a new population of baptized Jews virtually overnight. With the establishment of a Portuguese Inquisition in 1536, these conversos faced conditions similar to those in Spain. Yet the circumstances of the Portuguese Jews' conversion and exposure to the Inquisition were such that in Portugal judaizing was far more robust than in Spain.[22]

The perception that conversos' Jewish ancestry—their impure "blood"—predisposed them to judaize contributed to the racialization of identity in Iberian lands.[23] As a result, baptism lost its status as a sacrament that produced an essential change in the person receiving it. Even trained Catholic clerics were tempted to conclude—church teaching notwithstanding—that achieving the genuine conversion of persons with Jewish "blood" was virtually impossible.[24] It is true that Jewish converts to Christianity were viewed with suspicion wherever they lived, but in Iberian lands suspicion fell on countless persons baptized at birth and living as sincere Catholics, about whom the only cause for concern was their distant Jewish ancestry.

How exactly do conversos—whether sincere Catholics or judaizers—fit into a discussion of "conversion" in Jewish history? From late antiquity to the dawn of the modern period, the authority of rabbinic scholars to determine Jewish status was essentially unquestioned. But Iberian conversos—at least by the sixteenth century—lived in an environment in which the very existence of postbiblical Judaism was largely unrecognized, even among the most ardent judaizers.[25] Rabbinic authorities in Italy and North Africa were sometimes called on to rule on the status of conversos, usually in matters of marital status or inheritance. Yet their decisions were irrelevant to the conversos involved, with whom they had no contact; they mattered only to the relatives who lived openly as Jews outside the Iberian Peninsula.[26]

It was Church and crown that effectively determined the legal status of descendants of the forcibly converted Jews in Spain and Portugal. A single distant Jewish ancestor was enough to render someone a "converso" or "New Christian." Such a person was a member of what was euphemistically called "the Nation"—that is, the population of persons with Jewish ancestry of any degree. In Portugal, solidarity among conversos was reinforced by the fact that "the Nation" constituted a recognized corporate body.[27] Popularly, conversos were often referred to simply as "Jews" or the pejorative "*marranos*." Assimilated conversos used strategies to rid themselves of their unwanted special status and could sometimes purchase certificates of "purity of blood" attesting to their status as "Old Christians."

Judaizing conversos, however, embraced and celebrated their membership in "the Nation," refashioning the concept to make it their own. They could do this because the term "nation" resonated with the biblical concept of peoplehood. The Jewish Bible was available to educated judaizers in the form of the Latin Vulgate's Old Testament, which constituted a unique source of textual authority. The Bible also offered reassurance that conversos had not been cut off from the vital mainstream of Jewish history. Conversos used the term "captivity" to describe their predicament, which they saw as a replication of the fate of the Israelites in Egypt; as such, they were not marginal but key actors in divine history. They did not see themselves as anything less than authentic Jews, their baptism and cases of intermarriage among them notwithstanding.

Yet conversions—purely subjective ones—did take place, sometimes in dramatic fashion. On the one hand, conversos who initially judaized might choose to abandon their Jewish loyalties, finding a genuine spiritual home in Catholicism.[28] On the other, assimilated conversos might in adulthood turn fervently to "the Law of Moses." Such persons did not regard themselves as converts to Judaism. Their internalization of Iberian racial concepts and their sense of belonging to "the Nation" meant that they felt themselves always to have been Jews. Nevertheless, some conversos who underwent an inner turn to the Law of Moses felt a need to mark the transition from their existence as conforming Catholics to their new existence as Jews. The defining ritual among the most fervent was, for males, the highly risky act of self-circumcision (along with the adoption of a Hebrew name). A famous early case was that of the converso Diego Pires who, inspired by the visit to Portugal in 1525 by the messianic pretender David Reuveni, circumcised himself and took the name Solomon Molkho before fleeing Portugal.[29] Many decades later, the well-known judaizing martyrs Luis de Carvajal and Francisco Maldonado de Silva (whose mother was incidentally an Old Christian) marked their passage into active and ardent judaizing by taking the dangerous step of circumcising themselves, as well as adopting Jewish names.[30]

In rare instances, Old Christians, bitterly dissatisfied with Catholicism after their exposure to crypto-Jewish thinking—as well as to humanist and Protestant currents that dovetailed in important respects with crypto-judaizing—underwent ritualized self-conversions to Judaism. The most prominent such figure was the Spanish hidalgo Lope de Vera, who circumcised himself while in an inquisitorial prison and adopted the Hebrew name Judah, after which he declared himself to the warden to be a "judaizing Jew."[31] It is revealing that such self-conversions were viewed as perfectly authentic in normative Jewish communities established by converso emigres. The fact of never having undergone rabbinic conversion did not prevent either Lope de Vera or another Old Christian judaizing martyr, Diogo d'Assumpção, from becoming celebrated Jewish martyrs among the Portuguese Jews in Amsterdam.[32]

In the collective lore of converso resistance, both in Iberian judaizing circles and in the Portuguese Jewish diaspora, it was the educated, martyrdom-courting judaizing martyrs who—combative, proud of their intellectual prowess, eager for public notoriety, and aggressively uncompromising—gained talismanic status.[33] Yet in Iberian lands, in the absence of Jewish communal institutions and written traditions, women took on new roles of responsibility and leadership. As Renée Levine Melammed argued, "The private domain became the sole site tenable for continuing the [Jewish] tradition." Men in judaizing circles had lost their place in the synagogue and communal administration, where they had enjoyed positions of honor and responsibility. Inquisition documents reveal that in these circumstances women assumed roles as the chief transmitters of Jewish tradition in the household orbit where they were responsible for ritual life and the education of the young.[34]

Conversos who emigrated from Iberian lands and settled in Jewish communities in Italy, North Africa, and the Ottoman Empire—and later in France, the Netherlands, England, and the imperial territories of those countries—fit no existing rabbinic category. By the fifteenth century they could hardly be considered forced converts, because they had been baptized in infancy as a matter of course. Nor could those who had lived as assimilated Catholics be regarded as returning apostates, because they had never left normative Jewish life.[35] Communal leaders and rabbis in the Jewish communities where they settled, sensitive to the ex-conversos' complex history (and often sharing it), appear to have accepted as Jews almost anyone considered to be a member of "the Nation." A "don't ask, don't tell" policy seems to have been the norm, despite the not uncommon intermarriages in converso family genealogies. Remarkably, the wife of the physician and apologete Isaac Orobio de Castro, who settled with her husband in Amsterdam in the 1660s, was accepted as a Jew in the community without undergoing conversion, although she was known to be a Gentile.[36]

Portuguese Jewish emigres to "lands of freedom" naturally felt a need to mark their momentous passage into authentic Jewish life, even if they were already Jews in their own minds. It is not surprising that the primary ritual that served this purpose was circumcision—an act that possessed considerable symbolic power for conversos, who commonly viewed it as the Jewish equivalent of the sacrament of baptism.[37] Significantly, it was performed on them without subsequent immersion, thus distinguishing it from the circumcision required for *giyyur*. In the highly patriarchal culture of Portuguese Jews, women were presumably regarded as included in a ritual that could be seen as a family affair.[38] But the mythic stratum of converso discourse also featured a classic archetype of collective Jewish conversion that was gender inclusive and collectivized: The ex-converso "return" to rabbinic Judaism was viewed as a reenactment of the experience of the Israelites who, liberated from Egyptian slavery, took on the observance of the Law of Moses at Mt. Sinai.[39]

The collective aspect of ex-converso "return" did not preclude personal and sometimes agonized experiences of a kind once viewed by scholars as the very essence of "conversion." The theme of repentance for sins committed in an "old" life was common among ex-converso authors.[40] The seventeenth-century Amsterdam author Daniel Levi de Barrios described fervent emotions of repentance as part of his own inner spiritual transformation, using the explicit language of conversion: "I am so changed from my past life that I am at pains to recognize myself, and if I recognize myself, it is barely so, because of the memory of the sins that . . . haunt the soul You gave me. . . . In my longing for You I am already converted [*convertido*] into another."[41]

Although collective myth and individual soul searching could exist in harmony, the Iberian judaizing environment was also, given its lack of traditionally trained religious authorities, a breeding ground for nonconformist thinking. The idealized (and essentially male) image of the autonomous religious seeker, whose pure quest for the truth led him to Judaism, drew from a Reformation sensibility discussed earlier. This image shaped the careers and thinking of both judaizing martyrs in Iberian lands and ex-converso authors outside those lands.[42] With this conceptualization of conversion, the biblical model was not the collective transformation of the Israelites at Mt. Sinai but the lonely path taken by the patriarch Abraham.

In such an ethos, an emigre might reject rabbinic authority, adopt a "personal religion" untethered to established religious authority, and leave the Jewish community without joining another religious community. It is no coincidence that the earliest such challenges in the Jewish world came from within the Portuguese Jewish community of Amsterdam, a city where the government mostly did not interfere in matters of conscience. Spinoza is often accorded the status of pioneer in this respect: After his excommunication in 1656 he belonged to no religious community and adopted an entirely unique theological/political outlook. Quite different was the tragic case of Uriel da Costa, who consciously fashioned himself in the image of the lonely seeker, yet found he was unable to exist in isolation outside the community whose authority he vehemently rejected.[43]

For the most part, however, high-minded religious concerns were not paramount in determining the religious behavior of Portuguese Jews; emotional and practical considerations governed their choices. Some of them, having been immersed in both Catholic and Jewish environments, traveled on business or visited relatives in Iberian lands where of necessity they conducted themselves as Catholics—to the dismay of Jewish communal officials who imposed punishments on them as a condition for their full return to the community. Some ex-conversos returned permanently to Iberian lands out of disappointment with their new lives and nostalgia for their old. Still others developed a way of life as itinerant merchants trading between southern France, where they lived as Jews, and Iberian towns, where they adhered to Catholicism.[44] Here as in other aspects of converso life, conventional categories of apostasy and conversion hardly seem applicable; the complex dynamics of permanently unstable identities were at play.

Overall, although halakhic definitions of identity were enshrined in theory in the Portuguese Jewish diaspora, they were subordinated to the ethnocultural definition of "the Nation." Bound together by ancestry, Iberian culture, and historical experience, Portuguese Jews often found it difficult to feel part even of the wider Jewish world, with its Yiddish-speaking Ashkenazim and strange customs. Their particular and precarious sense of distinctiveness had implications for their attitudes to Gentile converts to Judaism. The very idea that a person with no Jewish ancestry could become a Jew through *giyyur* was incompatible with an outlook that privileged "blood." Seeking to harmonize rabbinic principles with converso assumptions, Orobio de Castro (whose wife, it may be remembered, was a Gentile) rejected the mainstream rabbinic notion that a person who underwent *giyyur* became a Jew in every respect. In his blunt formulation—which echoed a persistent rival strand of thought in Jewish tradition—he held that "Gentiles who acknowledge the true God and worship him will be converts within Israel and beloved of God, but they will never be Israelites nor of the seed of Abraham."[45]

Orobio was by no means alone. Iberian Gentiles were occasionally accepted as converts with relative ease because they shared an Iberian culture that was integral to identity as a member of "the Nation." However, non-Iberian Gentiles who sought *giyyur*, which they could do in Amsterdam despite the disapproval of the authorities, were likely to be turned away. Although a few non-Iberian converts did join the Portuguese Jewish community in Amsterdam, they found themselves living at the margins. Still lower in the social hierarchy were slaves who joined the community on their emancipation: They were stigmatized not only as proselytes but also as *negros* or *mulatos*.[46]

To be sure, circumstances differed from community to community, and norms in Amsterdam were not necessarily those in Portuguese Jewish communities everywhere. Yet in the fractured world of the "Men of the Nation," the lines that differentiated "Jew" and "Gentile" were often quite unsettled and could be crossed in radically different ways.

The Ottoman Empire and Sabbateanism

In early modern Ottoman communities, Jews converted to Islam for some of the same reasons they converted to Christianity: to free themselves from discrimination, to escape heavy special taxation, or to advance their careers at court. Jews who were taken captive in the Ottoman Mediterranean were at special risk for converting, making their ransom a priority for Jewish communities. Overall, conversion to Islam was a less fraught and weighty step than it was in Christian Europe. Jews who Islamized did not experience pressure to prove their religious commitment, and authorities often turned a blind eye to those who, despite the prohibition of doing so, reverted to Judaism. Jewish women who married Muslim men were not required to convert (though many chose to), attesting to a relatively relaxed Ottoman attitude to religious boundaries. Although in principle no Ottoman subject could convert to a religion other than Islam, the urge to do so was a distinct possibility in the multireligious Ottoman Empire. Some Ottoman Jews did convert to Christianity, especially in places where there was a large Greek Orthodox population, as in Izmir.[47]

As in Christian lands, some Jewish women under Islam saw apostasy as a way out of a problematic marriage, as cases that came before *shariah* courts in the Ottoman period attest. They could circumvent a husband who refused to grant a *get* by converting to Islam, whereupon as new Muslims they would immediately be divorced from their Jewish husbands. The *shariah* court would also allow them to claim their marriage portion (which a Jewish court would deny them), and they might remarry a Muslim man—possibly also a convert from Judaism. Although in such cases women might choose to convert to escape difficulties related to their position as women, Marc David Baer has warned against the tendency to overemphasize the agency they were thereby able to exercise. He noted that they could free themselves from predicaments in the Jewish orbit by converting to Islam, but in so doing they were subordinating themselves to another male-dominated structure.[48]

Apostasy in the Ottoman world is best remembered for the sensational events within the movement led by Sabbatai Zevi, a charismatic kabbalist with strong antinomian impulses whom many Jews throughout the diaspora believed, at least for a time, to be the messiah. In 1666, Sabbatai converted to Islam under threat of death at the Ottoman sultan's court in Adrianople.[49] Recently, a case has been made for situating this episode in the context of a pietistic awakening in the sultan's court that led to conversionist pressures on Jews.[50] Although Sabbatai's conversion disillusioned most of his followers, others were too deeply invested in the cosmic myth spun around him to give it up, and they clung to it by ascribing mythical meaning to his apostasy.[51] After his conversion to Islam, Sabbatai prevailed on some of his believers to follow suit, and in the decades after his death others followed their example. These "Ma'aminim" or Dönmeh, as they were known, practiced Islam publicly but formed tight-knit groups that privately adhered to Sabbatean beliefs. They did not, as is sometimes assumed, seek to practice Judaism secretly but cultivated a distinct identity and theology that in their view superseded rabbinic Judaism. They survived by forming an insular social structure that excluded non-Dönmeh. Living in the Ottoman Empire, they were largely ignored by the authorities. They disappeared in the twentieth century due to assimilation, intermarriage, and secularization.[52]

Sabbateanism evolved in a quite different way in Poland under the charismatic leadership of Jacob Frank. Although early in his career Frank had cultivated contacts with the Dönmeh in Ottoman lands, his conversion to Islam had little bearing on his subsequent career. In Poland, where by 1759 he had developed a strong following, he and his disciples developed a theology that had distinctly Christian and strong anti-talmudic elements. Frankists turned the Jewish community decisively against them when they affirmed blood libel accusations aimed at (traditional) Jews. When their position toward both the mainstream Jewish community and the Catholic Church became untenable, they were effectively coerced into conversion to Catholicism. An estimated three thousand Frankists (mainly poor and marginal Jews) were baptized between 1759 and 1764. Their mass conversion was unprecedented in that Jewish leaders, far from seeking to keep them within the fold, encouraged and welcomed their exit. Not all who left assimilated into Catholic society, however: Frankist communities continued to exist into the nineteenth century, although in a greatly attenuated form.[53]

Conclusion

It would be unwise to try to draw any general conclusions about conversion in early modern Jewish societies. Yet it appears that across diverse environments—Protestant Europe, the Iberian world, and the Ottoman Empire—conditions were created that led to the emergence of new clandestine and protean forms of religious life, producing novel patterns of conversion to and from Judaism. Alongside familiar cases of apostasy and *giyyur*, we find phenomena that fit neither one category nor the other: the accommodations of Iberian conversos to their anomalous situation; the often ambivalent "return" of ex-conversos to rabbinic Judaism; the unconventional attraction to Judaism of Gentile spiritual seekers inspired by Reformation currents; and the subversive, antinomian Sabbateanism that placed the Dönmeh and Frankists outside all established religious groups. These early modern deviations from classic models of entry into and exit from Jewish life hint at challenges that would face communal and rabbinic authorities in the modern period, when religio-ethnic boundaries would be yet more fluid and religious adherence even more a matter of individual choice.

6 Modern

THE FRACTURING OF RELIGIOUS AUTHORITY

In the long stretch from late antiquity to the nineteenth century, there was in principle only one rabbinically acceptable motivation for a Gentile to be accepted as a convert. Conversion was to be "for the sake of heaven"—that is, he or she was to be motivated by belief in the central tenets of Judaism, which entailed acceptance of the yoke of the commandments. An exemplary *ger* was a Gentile who, driven by a yearning for ultimate truths, rejected the perceived idolatrous or inauthentic beliefs of his or her tradition and turned to Judaism. In real life, of course, motivations could be a deal more complicated and varied. In certain circumstances rabbinic authorities made explicit exceptions to the rule, allowing for the *giyyur* of persons whose motivations were clearly not "for the sake of heaven"—as when Maimonides, choosing the lesser of two evils, permitted the conversion of a female slave kept as a concubine by a Jewish master so that they could marry (discussed in chapter 4). Exceptions to the rule could be tolerated because the number of converts to Judaism was demographically insignificant, and issues of *giyyur* were not entangled with burning contemporary controversies.

The modern period—for the purposes of this study, from the mid-eighteenth to the mid-twentieth century—brought a radical shake-up to centuries-old patterns. Change was by no means uniform. Developments differed from place to place and among different sectors of Jewish society—elite and non-elite, male and female, urban and rural. Yet modernity had certain dominant features. This chapter focuses on conversion primarily in the geographical space where modernization trends were most intense and where scholars have concentrated their attention—Europe and the United States.

The transformations of the modern period have been explored exhaustively and need no elaboration here. Still, a brief discussion will help explain why the emphasis in this section is on apostasy. Well before the French Revolution ushered in the era of Jewish emancipation, the structures that for centuries kept European Jews anchored in an autonomous community began eroding. As early as the seventeenth century the social controls exercised by communal leaders over individual Jews weakened as modern centralizing governments began stripping the community of its coercive powers. In the same period, early signs of religious skepticism appeared, notably among the Portuguese Jews of Amsterdam, where Baruch Spinoza's challenge to rabbinic authority, although notorious, was by no means unique. Eventually the rationalist attack on rabbinic tradition made inroads among other European Jews. Whether or not they enjoyed full legal emancipation in the states where they lived, Europe's Jews were increasingly assimilated into mainstream society, first in western Europe and then gradually in central and eastern Europe. They enrolled in universities, moved into professions from which they had previously been excluded, and entered political life.

It was at this point that the secular Jew, fully detached from the Jewish community and confidently rooted in European culture, emerged as a social type. Secular and assimilated Jews were still exposed to antisemitism, whether in the form of subtle social exclusion or in new virulent expressions. But their access to institutions and workplaces from which they had once been excluded meant that they were able to mix with Gentiles as never before. In this environment, increasing numbers of Jews married non-Jews, abandoned traditional observance, or did both.

German Jewry was situated at the vortex of change. By the early nineteenth century, it was in full crisis. In 1819 the Jewish salon hostess Rahel Varnhagen wrote (with some exaggeration) that in the previous thirty years half of Berlin Jewry had converted to Christianity.[1] For Jewish leaders the torrent of defections from the community seemed catastrophic. The Berlin Haskalah (Jewish Enlightenment) movement of the 1780s, which sought to revitalize Judaism along European Enlightenment lines, had by this time lost its vitality. The chronic frustration of emancipation hopes among Berlin's wealthy Jews (which deepened as reaction set in after the French Revolution), on the one hand, and the social mixing of these Jews with Gentiles in Berlin's brilliant intellectual milieu, on the other, contributed to what was referred to as a *Taufepidemie*—a "baptism epidemic." The romantic valorization of instinct and feeling in the early nineteenth century undercut traditional communal and familial loyalties, so that a Jew's baptism was less likely to be experienced or viewed as betrayal.[2] Outside elite circles, poorer Jews also converted, primarily to escape restrictions that showed no signs of abating.

In an environment of collapsing traditional structures, the Jewish family became destabilized, with increasing rates of divorce, births outside marriage, and baptisms for the sake of intermarriage.[3] Baptisms for the sake of advancement were also an everyday occurrence. Heinrich Heine, a secular Jew through and through, nevertheless chose to be baptized, famously characterizing his conversion as his "entrance ticket to European culture." Some Jews sought new forms of religious inspiration and, under the sway of romantic values, found in Christianity a spirituality that was lacking, as they saw it, in the dry talmudic legalism of Jewish tradition. It was a hallmark of the new conditions that had emerged, however, that baptism was not required to survive outside the community. Some Jews, having grown apathetic to organized religion in general, chose to live without any affiliation to a faith-based community.

A new generation of university-educated German Jewish rabbis acted to stem the tide of defection. Adopting a modern scholarly outlook, they sought to create new structures of Jewish life that were more compatible with modern sensibilities. They served congregants whose aesthetic expectations were German, who favored universal values, and who no longer found meaning in Jewish ritual life. In the 1840s these rabbis, under the leadership of Abraham Geiger, broke definitively with the traditional rabbinic establishment—which from this point onward we can identify as "Orthodox"—and laid the foundations of Reform Judaism. In contrast to strict traditionalists, who continued to believe that the classical methods of rabbinic discourse were sufficient to deal with changing circumstances, Reform rabbis felt morally impelled by the historical change they were witnessing to apply a new standard of reasoning to establishing the norms of Jewish life. They hotly debated whether even such core practices as circumcision or prayer in the Hebrew language should be required.

For some reformers, Geiger's radicalism threatened to destroy essential features of Jewish tradition. They committed themselves to what Zachariah Fraenkel called "positive-historical Judaism." This was shorthand for a conception of Judaism that maintained the general validity of halakha, particularly practices that had been revered by pious Jews over the centuries, while at the same time subjecting it to modification by means of historical reasoning. Fraenkel's outlook would provide the intellectual and spiritual groundwork for the Conservative movement.

Out of this ferment, as two new movements established institutions and proved their viability, there emerged a new socioreligious structure, one in which Jews could choose under whose religious leadership and authority (if any) they wished to live. This created an unprecedented new set of issues in the realm of *giyyur*.

Conversion for Marriage

In nineteenth-century Germany where these developments began, few non-Jews had a desire to convert to Judaism. Indeed, conversion to Judaism was prohibited in some German states. Issues of *giyyur* might thus seem to have been of negligible importance. Yet the growing incidence of intermarriage created a new reality. Observers began to view the high incidence of baptism, intermarriage, and assimilation as posing an existential demographic threat.[4] There was increasing recognition that *giyyur* had a role to play in the fight to ensure Jewish survival. Simply writing off a Jew who chose to marry "out" as lost to the Jewish community was to ignore the complexities. A secular Jew might well give romantic love priority over Jewish loyalties by choosing a Gentile partner but, at the same time, might feel impelled by those loyalties to establish a Jewish home. The Gentile partner, for her part (and it was typically a woman), might want to be fully accepted by her husband's Jewish family and create a harmonious ethos in the home; she might even have an appreciation for Jewish customs and values. If so, she might be willing to undergo *giyyur*. But if she were to be turned away by a rabbinic court because her motivations were not primarily "for the sake of heaven," what then would she and her partner do? Might they not, feeling spurned, find a welcoming home in Christianity? If this happened, the Jewish community would lose both the Jewish spouse and the couple's children. If, however, the Gentile partner was accepted for conversion because, in her own way, she wanted to be a Jew, her *giyyur* might contribute to ensuring the preservation of a Jewish religious and historical consciousness, however attenuated.

Orthodox halakhists regarded the time-tested methods of rabbinic deliberation both as sufficient to meet the exigencies of the age and as essential to maintaining the sanctity of tradition. But they were not of one mind. Many adopted an unyielding stance and flatly prohibited the conversion of a Gentile for whom conversion was ancillary to marriage. They relied on a chain of major rulings going back to a key passage in the Talmud invalidating conversion for the sake of marriage (Yevamot 24b). The *Shulkhan Arukh* moreover codified a requirement to actively investigate a potential convert's motivation, calling on the *beit din* involved to probe whether a romantic attachment was the incentive: "Perhaps he placed his eyes on a Jewish woman," or "perhaps she placed her eyes on the single men of Israel."[5] If this was the case, the potential convert was to be turned away. Halakhists who insisted on strictly following this ruling were not simply acting on an instinctive resistance to the dangers that modernity posed, although that surely played a role. For them the very essence of Jewishness remained a commitment to halakha. Because it was evident that most of those converting for marriage would not live as halakhically observant Jews, they could find no justification for their conversion. The Galician rabbinic authority Zvi Hirsch Chajes opined that strict application of this rule had to be defended even if it meant that some Jews would abandon Jewish life.[6]

Yet methods of halakhic discourse had always provided room for creative interpretation. A much-cited ruling that reflected a more flexible stance was that of Shlomo Kluger, an influential rabbinic scholar in mid-nineteenth-century Brody. A local *beit din* sought a ruling from Kluger on the eligibility for *giyyur* of a Gentile woman who was in a relationship with a Jew. The two had fallen in love while the Jew was serving in the army and wanted to marry. Employing a bit of exegetical ingenuity, Kluger ruled that the woman was in fact eligible for conversion, using the very conceptual language other rabbis might have used to turn her away. He held that she should not be regarded as someone who was seeking *giyyur* only "to obtain a man," because, in this case, she already *had* a man. The couple could have formalized their union by having the man undergo baptism and marrying as Christians. But, Kluger reasoned, because they wanted to marry as Jews, with the woman converting to Judaism, "it is proven that their intention is 'for the sake of heaven.'"[7]

What Kluger seems to have meant by "for the sake of heaven" in this responsum was simply the preference of the person seeking conversion to belong to a Jewish community when other (perhaps easier) choices were available. But regardless of how he construed the phrase, Kluger's responsum reflected accommodation to an overall shift in the nature of religious affiliation in modern life. In contrast to premodern societies where religion was an integral aspect of a person's identity in a corporately structured society, religious affiliation in modern societies was often viewed as a matter of individual choice. Kluger's ruling, and subsequent rulings in the same vein by other halakhists, reflected a recognition in some Orthodox quarters of the need to adapt to an unprecedented sociological and human reality.[8] Within the Orthodox rabbinic orbit, however, the issue remained (and remains) a contested one.

The Reform movement charted its own course on issues of *giyyur*, establishing criteria for accepting potential converts that conformed to its interpretation of Judaism and reassessing the established ritual requirements. Inevitably, this led to conflict. In the 1860s, for example, a controversy broke out when the ardent reformer Adolf Jellinek performed the wedding of a Jew and a woman whose conversion Abraham Geiger had overseen. At issue was the fact that Geiger had not required the woman to immerse in a ritual bath as part of the conversion. Both Azriel Hildesheimer, a pioneer of modern Orthodoxy, and Moritz Güdemann, a graduate of the Breslau Jewish Theological Seminary founded by Zachariah Fraenkel, ruled that the marriage was invalid.[9] This early dispute, which threatened the traditional consensus about who was a Jew, foreshadowed a key area of future discord.

Reform, Conservative, and Orthodox: The American Scene

Issues related to *giyyur* arose in the United States well before the Reform movement took root there. They resulted from conditions of Jewish life in early America, in which several factors led to a high incidence of intermarriage: a sparse Jewish population in rural areas, a highly acculturated Jewish population in urban areas, weak communal controls, and the absence of rabbinic authorities who could make definitive rulings. Synagogue boards might decide on their own when issues arose, such as whether the child of a Jewish father and non-Jewish mother could be ritually circumcised. Or Jewish communal authorities could send queries to European halakhists, despite the long wait needed for a reply. It was apparently rare, however, to require a couple to wait for a ruling from Europe approving the conversion of a non-Jewish spouse.[10] In the 1780s two board members of a Philadelphia congregation wrote to a rabbinic scholar in Amsterdam complaining about the situation "in this country where everyone does as he pleases."[11]

This situation changed in the mid-nineteenth century, when leading Reform rabbis from Germany began settling in the United States. They quickly established Reform as the major form of organized Jewish life and adopted an increasingly radical program. In 1869, at the Reform Conference in Philadelphia, Isaac Mayer Wise made the conversion of men less onerous by holding that male converts should not be required to undergo circumcision. David Einhorn objected, arguing that converts should be required to do so to prevent an influx of undesirable persons into the Jewish community. But he was fighting a losing battle: In 1892 the movement's principal organization, the Central Conference of American Rabbis, ruled that converts could be accepted "without any initiatory rite, ceremony or observance whatever."[12] Reform leaders also parted ways with the traditional resistance to proselytization by encouraging outreach to non-Jewish spouses in mixed civil marriages—a policy that has been normative in the movement to this day.

The Conservative movement in the United States, which had its origins in resistance to Reform, continued to regard as unnegotiable the classic talmudic ritual procedures by which non-Jews were inducted into Jewish life—that is, appearance before a *beit din*, circumcision or *hatafat dam* for male converts, immersion, and acceptance of halakha as determined by their rabbis. Some Conservative rabbis apparently accepted Reform conversions after the fact. However, in 1940 the movement's Law Committee ruled that without immersion a woman converted by a Reform rabbi would not be recognized as a Jew.[13] Rulings in the 1980s further confirmed the movement's requirement that *giyyur* be conducted according to Conservative halakha.[14] This position might seem to have been virtually indistinguishable from that of the Orthodox. However, Orthodox rabbis rejected Conservative conversions on the grounds both that Conservative rabbinic courts had no authority and that the Conservative program to educate potential converts was inadequate.

The situation created by conflicting requirements for conversion was historically novel and challenged a cardinal value in Jewish tradition: the preservation of Jewish unity. In earlier periods, the legitimacy of a conversion performed by a valid *beit din* was taken for granted and accepted in communities throughout the Jewish diaspora. Under the new conditions, in which there were divergent criteria for the acceptance of converts, a person who underwent *giyyur* in one denominational community, and who was fully recognized as a Jew in that community, would not necessarily have the status of a Jew in another. The impact, moreover, was multigenerational: Descendants of women whose conversions were not accepted by Orthodox or Conservative rabbis would be regarded in those streams as Gentiles. Because most converts were women, it was they who were most often faced with the non-acceptance of their conversions and the Jewishness of their children in Orthodox or Conservative quarters.

Overall, the voluntaristic character of Jewish communal life in the United States, where Jewish life is conducted mainly within the bounds of a person's denominational community, has served to mitigate issues around *giyyur*. Converts integrated as a matter of course into the life of the communities in which they converted. Yet certain situations have made conversion a site of contention, exposing to view discord over the definition of Jewish/Gentile boundaries. Most frequently this has occurred when an Orthodox or Conservative rabbi has been asked to preside at the wedding of a convert whose conversion they deem invalid. In such cases, the convert has had to undergo a second conversion.[15] Cases of this sort test the pastoral skills of the rabbi, who must deal not only with the conceptual incongruity of a second conversion but also with the convert's distress.

Even in death the convert's status has sometimes been contested. According to halakha, non-Jews cannot be buried in Jewish cemeteries. Yet Jewish cemeteries typically serve all denominations. Given the heightened sensitivity of this matter, Orthodox halakhists have in effect given a quasi-Jewish status—for the purposes of burial only—to Conservative and Reform converts, taking into consideration the fact that such converts, although not Jews by Orthodox standards, have identified as Jews and taken part in Jewish life. At the same time, they have drawn a line of sorts, ruling that Orthodox burials be carried out at a certain distance from the graves of non-Orthodox converts.[16]

Religiously Driven Conversion

It can easily be overlooked that conversions to Judaism undertaken in anticipation of marriage (which constituted the overwhelming majority of cases in the nineteenth and twentieth centuries) might also have a spiritual aspect, even if that aspect is ancillary to forming a family with a common identity and way of life. Confidence in the spiritual attractiveness of their own universalistic vision of Judaism was part of the calculus when American Reform leaders broke with traditional Jewish policy and called for the active proselytization of Gentile marriage partners.[17] Yet individuals who came forward with a purely spiritual interest in Judaism—that is, without marriage in mind—have not always been greeted with open arms. Some of the most liberal-minded American Reform rabbis expressed reluctance to accept such converts. According to the historian Jacob Rader Marcus, this was because, "when the cards were down, most Jewish Reform rabbis were also ethnicists"; that is, they were socially insular like their congregants, and the peculiar phenomenon of a Gentile who chose to be a Jew made them uncomfortable. Some such attitude would seem to have been at work when in 1896 the Virginia Reform rabbi

Edward Nathan Calisch (under the advice of his Chicago rabbinic mentor Emil Hirsch) rejected the earnest application for conversion of a man who had once studied to be a Congregationalist minister but who hoped with his newfound Jewish convictions to study at Hebrew Union College.[18]

Certainly, converts with strong spiritual motivations sometimes posed genuine problems. Their insistence on seeing things their own way could be instrumental in driving them to embrace a stigmatized religion in the first place, but it might also render difficult their integration into a Jewish community that needed to carefully negotiate its minority position. Such a problematic figure was the notorious late eighteenth-century Scottish aristocrat Lord George Gordon. Gordon had formed positive attitudes about Israelites and Jewish Scripture early in his career, under the sway of Scottish philosemitic traditions and Protestant millenarianism. His colorful, erratic later career in religiously infused radical politics brought him into contact with Jews associated with Scottish Rite Masonry, including the kabbalistic wonder-worker Samuel Falk, who may have influenced Gordon's inner conversion to Judaism sometime after 1785. Given Gordon's provocative political activity and his extravagant religiosity, it is not surprising that his request to the London rabbi Tevele Schiff to be formally converted was turned down. Yet he did subsequently undergo a prescribed ritual conversion, the details of which are obscure. Contemporaries commented on his strict and somewhat ostentatious Jewish observance from 1787 until his death in prison in 1793.[19]

Nineteenth-century Protestant millenarianism was similarly at play in the remarkable career of the American convert Warder Cresson. Born into a Philadelphia Quaker family, Cresson came of age in a period of religious revival. His dissatisfaction with what he saw as the spiritual and social shortcomings of the Quakers led him to search elsewhere. Beginning in the 1840s, he developed a spiritual kinship with Isaac Leeser, an important American Jewish religious leader and publicist who appealed in his writings to Christians as well as Jews. An equally significant figure in Cresson's development was the proto-Zionist (or more accurately, Jewish restorationist) Mordecai Manuel Noah, whose ideas about the advantageous geopolitical alignment in the Middle East and the possibility of Jewish agricultural settlement in Palestine excited Cresson's imagination. By 1844 Cresson was in Jerusalem, eager to witness the coming restoration. By 1847 he chose to be identified by a Jewish name. He was circumcised and converted in 1848 before returning to Philadelphia, where his wife and other family members had him put on trial on charges of insanity. He was eventually acquitted after a widely publicized defense in which his lawyer challenged the prosecution's implication that conversion to Judaism was evidence of a psychiatric condition. Cresson returned to the Holy Land where he established an agricultural settlement in Emek Refaim in Jerusalem, promoting a form of labor that he viewed as intrinsic to the redemptive process.[20]

These two admittedly unusual cases (they are well documented for that reason) are not meant to be representative. Indeed, they underscore the absence of a thorough, synthetic study of *giyyur* in the modern period. Yet they suggest continuity with a general pattern, one with parallels in medieval and early modern times, in which Old Testament themes and prophecies, viewed through the filter of contemporary concerns, raised questions among religiously driven Christians about the validity of their beliefs and produced an emotional identification with Jews and Jewish tradition.

Apostasy to Christianity

Studies of Jewish apostasy in the modern era have focused almost entirely (like research on modern Jewish history in general) on developments in Europe and America, where it is estimated that several hundred thousand Jews were baptized.[21] The conditions in which Jews chose baptism had undergone considerable change by the modern period. No longer was the distinction so sharp between the vast majority of Jews for whom Jewish communal life was a given and the few who abandoned Jewish life for a different faith community. The Jewish population could now better be viewed along a socioreligious continuum. At one extreme were those Jews who remained deeply enmeshed in insular Orthodox Jewish communities; at the other were those who underwent a passionate conversion to Christianity. In between were significant numbers of Jews who related in a wide variety of ways to their Jewishness. They might be affiliated with modern Orthodox or Liberal congregations; they might live as secular Jews, participating (or not) in Jewish organizational activity; they might undergo baptism for the sake of marriage or career while remaining indifferent to any religious tradition. Jews in modern liberal states also had the option of entirely abandoning the Jewish world and passing as Gentiles—perhaps even attending an Episcopalian or Presbyterian church—without formally joining a non-Jewish faith group.[22] In representing conversion in such an environment, it is somewhat artificial to draw a distinction between formal conversion "out" and thoroughgoing assimilation. Demonstrating how closely related these two phenomena could be, Todd Endelman has advanced the concept of "radical assimilation" to include the entire array of avenues of escape from Jewish life that modern conditions have offered.[23]

The erosion of old boundaries led some important rigorist Orthodox rabbis in the early days of the Reform movement to insist on a newly defined sharp boundary, with the Orthodox on one side and all other persons of Jewish origin on the other. Reform had scarcely appeared on the scene when, in 1819, the Pressburg rabbi Moses Schreiber ("Hatam Sofer"), a leading Orthodox rabbi in central Europe and an uncompromising opponent of Reform, wrote that "their sect should be considered like those of Zadok and Boethus, Anan, and Saul [ben Anan]"—infamous sectarians in Jewish historical memory.[24] In the 1840s, Galician rabbi Zvi Hirsch Chajes and Halberstadt rabbi Mattathias Levian both explicitly referred to the Reformers as *mumarim*, or apostates. They and others made halakhic decisions accordingly: One was not to visit Reform Jews in their homes or mourn them at their deaths.[25] Even the more moderate rabbinic scholar Azriel Hildesheimer adopted the view that Reformers were apostates and should be treated as such (although he modified this position later in his career). Only the rise of antisemitism in Germany after 1870 led Jews to abandon this posture, and Orthodox Jews joined forces with the Liberals to fight the onslaught of propaganda. By the end of the nineteenth century, Jews of all orientations had come to recognize the reality of a fractured Jewish community, with competing structures of authority and allegiance.[26]

In the heterogeneous socioreligious world of modern Jews, the way Jewish baptism was perceived underwent modification, at least in some quarters. It had always been the case that Jews continued to interact to some degree with coreligionists who apostatized. However, in the past Jews and apostates had belonged to separate communities with distinct modes of dress, speech, and behavior—communities whose boundaries were policed by church and state authorities, as well as by the leaders of the autonomous Jewish community. Moreover, a pervasive religious ethos tended to heighten the Jewish perception of baptism as an act of betrayal. In modern societies, in contrast, it was no longer clear that baptized Jews had abandoned one existence and adopted another. Attuned to life in an individualistic society, a secular Jew might well accept the conversion of a fellow Jew with something of a shrug, at least if the baptism had been clearly transactional. The guilty party in such cases was not so much the convert who abandoned Judaism but rather the liberal society that had failed to eradicate antisemitism. (This was underscored when converts to Christianity defended Jews and Judaism against attack.[27]) The pragmatic quality of so many baptisms, which some converts openly admitted, gave rise to a minor genre of Jewish humor. The Russian Jewish scholar Daniel Kvolson, when asked if he had converted from conviction, famously replied that it was indeed a matter of conviction—his conviction that being a scholar in St. Petersburg was better than being a melamed in Eyshishok.[28]

This is not to say that the social acceptance of baptized Jews implied approval of their apostasy or that such acceptance was universal. Even the scholar of Jewish mysticism Gershom Scholem's quite assimilated father regarded baptism as "an unprincipled and servile act."[29] Communal leaders alarmed by the loss to the community denounced it. Especially among religious and nationalist Jews, apostasy was viewed as an unforgivable betrayal. Sholem Aleichem's warm-hearted character Tevye the Milkman chastised himself, after his daughter Chava converted to marry a Russian peasant, for his inability to respond as he felt he should—by completely tearing his daughter from his heart.[30]

The variability in conditions from one Jewish milieu to another meant variability in the patterns of conversion. Converts differed widely in their socioeconomic backgrounds, motivations, and behaviors. In nineteenth-century Germany, for example, university-educated, affluent Berlin Jews were more likely to convert than provincial German Jews who lived in a more insular social milieu.[31] Yet in the American west where Jews were scattered and lived in non-Jewish environments, or in provincial towns and villages of the Pale of Settlement where Jews came into everyday contact with Gentiles as innkeepers, soldiers, and shopkeepers, converts typically stemmed from the lower ranks and generally wed equally low-status Gentile partners.[32]

The irregular patterns of apostasy are nicely illustrated by studies of gender differences, which were especially pronounced in contexts where women were exposed to modernizing trends in a way that men were not. Novel trends of this kind first appeared in the privileged and wealthy stratum of Berlin Jews in Enlightenment Germany. Men were typically prepared for careers in the traditionally Jewish realm of commerce and finance, whereas women were encouraged to engage in the cultural pursuits of the Gentile elite. Several wealthy Jewish salonières in this milieu converted, and these high-profile cases attracted considerable attention. Their conversions may have been interpreted by contemporary male observers as evidence of female shallowness,[33] but contemporary scholars point to the important role in their conversions of the conflicts inherent in their upbringing. Often unhappy in their arranged marriages to men who had a conventional Jewish education, these women, who were genuinely attracted to Enlightenment thought (or, somewhat later, romantic spirituality), found they could achieve through conversion and marriage to a Gentile "integration into the dominant upper-class culture and society, the model of civilized humanity."[34] For a time, in light of these circumstances, female conversions in Berlin outnumbered male conversions. Yet as middle- and upper-class men sought to enter the professions and arts—careers that were closed to unbaptized Jews—they soon caught up with women.[35]

Although the Berlin Jewish community has held a particularly prominent place in modern Jewish historiographical consciousness, its patterns of apostasy, given its idiosyncratic demography, were hardly representative. Over the long nineteenth century, it was most often poor and middle-class Jews who chose baptism, and gender patterns varied widely. In Jewish communities where women were mostly occupied in the home and had few opportunities to meet non-Jewish men, conversion was more frequent among men, who routinely met non-Jewish women in the workplace. However, once lower- and lower-middle class women entered the workforce, the disparity tended to disappear. Indeed, in some places, Vienna and Breslau among them, low-status female converts far outnumbered male converts.[36]

Although the diversity of patterns makes it difficult to generalize, scholars point to certain common themes. A study of late nineteenth-century Cracow is a case in point. There, most converts were young women from fifteen to twenty years old. They grew up in villages and small towns in western Galicia, where they received a Polish education and lived in an overwhelmingly non-Jewish environment. (Their conversions were registered in Cracow because they went there to convert.) The gender gap has been explained by the fact that, in contrast to the girls, Jewish boys in the villages of Galicia were raised in a way that emphasized their Jewish identity and commitments. They attended a traditional Jewish school (*heder*), whereas girls attended government primary schools for which the curriculum sought to inculcate an appreciation for Polish culture.[37] Todd Endelman has pointed to structural parallels to the situation in Berlin a century earlier: "The daughters of Berlin bankers at the start of the nineteenth century and the daughters of Galician tavern-keepers at the end of the century shared a similar predicament, having received a secular education that fired their imaginations and alienated them from conventional Jewish society and its norms."[38]

Although most baptisms were motivated by a striving for social, economic, and cultural benefits—and although calculations of personal gain can never be discounted as accompanying factors—there were baptized Jews in the modern period whose pivotal experience was a religious awakening of a kind associated with classic conceptualizations of "conversion." Among these were members of an educated, assimilated circle in early to mid- nineteenth-century France who became fervent Catholics, apparently swept up in the romantic sensibility of the time. Two of them, the brothers Théodore and Alphonse Ratisbonne, became fierce polemicists against a Judaism they knew primarily through Catholic teaching. It is no accident that Alphonse Ratisbonne's intense description of his conversion experience crops up in William James's seminal study of religious conversion.[39]

Modern apostates, not unlike some of their premodern predecessors, were sometimes heavily involved in missionary work. A religious awakening in eighteenth-century Britain and Germany led to the establishment of several organizations that specialized in evangelizing Jews, the best known of which was the London Society for Promoting Christianity among the Jews, an organization that was active in central and eastern Europe, the Balkans, North Africa, and the Middle East. The tactics of these groups offended the sensibilities of most Jews, as did the participation of erstwhile coreligionists in their work. In practice, these organizations proved resoundingly ineffective. They reached mainly the poor and uprooted and were known to draw misfits and swindlers. The brother of a Düsseldorf missionary noted, "The harvest yield was very small and the effort, work, and costs very great."[40]

Fears aroused by mounting antisemitism were more likely than missionary activity to precipitate Jewish conversions. The period between 1870 and World War I saw a sharp rise in antisemitic rhetoric, discrimination, and political agitation in Europe and America; it was accompanied by a sharp rise in the number of Jewish conversions. The rise of Nazism led to a further spike, with desperate acts of baptism that were usually of no avail.[41] Although a few survivors and refugees chose baptism in the wake of the Holocaust, and although Jewish orphans who had been baptized by Christian couples who took them in often chose to remain in the religion of their protectors, the changed conditions of the postwar period meant that baptism was no longer a useful means to escape persecution or discrimination.[42]

The coerced conversion of Jews was rare in the modern period and never unfolded on the scale of the major medieval episodes, but it did occur. Two European episodes stand out. In both cases reactionary rulers (a tsar and a pope, respectively) took actions to impose Christianity on Jewish minors. In the Russian case, the conversions were part of a wider campaign of coercive Russification of minorities. From 1827 to 1856, Jewish boys, some as young as eight years old, were conscripted into the Russian army, with the Jewish community forced into the role of supplying the recruits. One of the aims of recruiting these young "cantonists," as they were known, was to bring about their conversion by separating them from their families and communities and depriving them of access to the most basic elements of Jewish tradition. It is estimated that under these conditions between 15,000 and 20,000 Jewish children were baptized into the Russian Orthodox Church.[43] The missionizing ex-cantonist Alexander Alekseev recalled having assisted in the mass baptism of more than a hundred Jewish cantonists in the Volga River, an event memorialized in a painting sent to the War Ministry and the tsar.[44]

The second case involved only a few individuals but gained wide public attention. By the nineteenth century, the reach of the papacy's power extended no farther than the boundaries of the papal states in Italy. However, because in those states he was sovereign, the pope was able to act in defiance of norms that were by then accepted throughout western Christendom. Thus in 1858 the Vatican sent its police to seize the six-year-old Jewish boy Edgardo Mortara from his family in Bologna, based on a report that a servant woman had baptized him as an infant when she thought he was mortally ill. The church in theory prohibited baptisms of infants against the will of their parents, but once performed such baptisms could not be invalidated. Despite international protests, Pope Pius IX refused to restore the boy to his family, holding that the baptism was valid and the boy was a Catholic. (Under the tutelage of the church, Edgardo Mortara eventually became an ordained priest.[45]) The Mortara case, although the most sensational of its kind, was by no means unique.[46]

Apostasy and Forcible Conversion to Islam

In Muslim lands in the modern period where Jews retained the traditional status of dhimmis and where secularization was not a significant factor, Jews converted to Islam for many of the reasons that historically motivated Jews to adopt the majority religion: poverty, thwarted social and career aspirations, romantic attachments to non-Jews, marital or other family problems, and the opportunity to escape criminal punishment.[47] Yet overall, insofar as the few existing studies indicate, apostasy was rare and unremarkable. The process of conversion to Islam was, as noted earlier, a simple one. (In Yemen, the convert's passage from the Jewish community to Islam included, along with the recitation of the *shahada* and the adoption of a Muslim name, eating a soup made with meat slaughtered according to Islamic law—a ritual unique to Yemen.[48]) In Islamic law, the return of proselytes to their former religious community was prohibited. Yet Jewish apostates sometimes moved to a different town to revert to Judaism, thereby escaping the notice of the Muslim authorities; in other cases, the authorities turned a blind eye to their return. When they were received back into the Jewish community, some returnees were subjected to (or requested) penance, whereas others returned to Jewish life without ceremony.[49]

Under Islam, Jews were generally not subjected to the kinds of pressures that led to radical assimilation in Europe and the United States. An apparently exceptional episode in this respect occurred in 1930s and 1940s Iraq. After World War I, there emerged a group of Iraqi Jewish intellectuals who had been educated in Europe or Turkey and whose secularized outlook placed them increasingly outside the Jewish community. Among them were writers and poets who wrote in Arabic, who identified with the Islamic legacy, and who were drawn to Iraqi nationalism or pan-Arabism. A striking figure among them was the writer Ahmad Nissim Susa, who had been educated at the American University in Beirut and the University of Chicago. Susa converted to Islam in 1936 and wrote a two-volume work describing his path to Islam. He maintained that a Jew could not espouse the Arab cause without renouncing Judaism and Zionism. The cultivation of such an outlook among Iraqi Jews was, however, as short-lived as it was confined to elite circles. In the early 1940s a group of Iraqi Jewish intellectuals flirted with the idea of converting to Islam but abandoned the idea as Nazi propaganda gained a foothold in Iraqi society.[50] The extensive persecution of Iraqi Jews in the wake of the establishment of the State of Israel, leading to their mass emigration, spelled a definitive end to any such assimilatory aspirations.

By the modern period, forced conversions under threat of violence were quite exceptional in Muslim lands and unknown under Ottoman rule. In Iran, anti-Jewish riots in 1839 led to the forced mass conversion of Jews in the towns of Shiraz and Mashhad. The Shiraz Jews were allowed to return to the open practice of Judaism some years later, and many of the Mashhadi Jews fled across the border to places where they could return to Judaism. However, a group of Mashhadi Jews lived for decades as *Jadid al-Islam* (New Muslims), for the most part without having to rigorously conceal their continued adherence to Judaism. Their fate and status after 1948 are discussed briefly in chapter 9, "'Emerging' Jews."[51]

Conclusion

In places where modernity brought rapid changes to the conditions of Jewish life, the traditional norms governing how Gentiles might become Jews faced fundamental challenges. Jewish communal and rabbinic authorities, confronting sharply increasing numbers of intermarriages, were forced to rethink those norms. Authorities in all sectors of Jewish communal life made adaptations to modern realities, but they differed substantially one from another, creating an unprecedented situation in which conversions in one community were liable to be rejected in another, threatening the unity of the Jewish world. Although the number of converts to Judaism reached unprecedented levels, significant numbers of assimilating Jews chose to leave the Jewish world. Some were content to live as secular, religiously unaffiliated citizens; for others, baptism offered the hope of escape from stigma, restrictions, and antisemitism—and for a few, spiritual fulfillment.

PART II

STATE OF THE QUESTION

7 *State of Israel*

In the decades after the end of World War II, the single most significant development for practices and thinking around *giyyur* was the establishment of the State of Israel. In the postwar diaspora—as was the case earlier—Orthodox, Conservative, and Reform leaders charted their own respective courses largely independently of each other, free to do so in countries that as a matter of principle did not interfere in matters of religion. In the new State of Israel, however, a very different model prevailed. From the outset, a state-mandated religious authority was given responsibility for the conduct of *giyyur*. As a result, issues around *giyyur*, which had historically been of little importance, became closely tied up with burning controversies around state and religion. Not only the state-mandated religious courts but other state agencies also became involved, including the Jewish Agency, the Ministry of Religious Affairs, and the Education Ministry.

Ideological differences fueled the tensions that periodically flared up. The Zionists who dominated public discourse reimagined the very contours of *giyyur*, giving it a role in the state-building mission. The ultra-Orthodox stood in passionate opposition, protesting what seemed to them the upending of classical rabbinic norms. Yet they, too, in their own way, modified those norms, demanding from converts an unprecedented adherence to halakha in all its detail.

Let me sketch the unfolding of developments. In the early years of the state, given the high priority Israeli leaders placed on preserving national unity and the fear of a split between religious and secular camps, a compromise was hammered out between secular and religious political parties on issues that included conversion. The "status quo agreement" of 1947—so called because it was a perpetuation of the arrangement under Ottoman and British rule—officially recognized the exclusive authority of the Orthodox Chief Rabbinate in the realm of personal status law, that is, in the areas of marriage, divorce, and conversion. The Chief Rabbinate alone could decide whose conversions would be accepted as valid by the state. Yet the opinions of rabbinic authorities were not uniform. Some of the Religious Zionist rabbis who filled positions in the state religious bureaucracy were sensitive to the needs of the state, advocating leniency in cases that involved mixed marriage. But the status quo agreement, even though aimed at achieving unity, ultimately contained the seeds of discord.

In the same early years of the state, soon after its establishment in 1948 when it was absorbing massive immigration from both post-Holocaust Europe and Arab countries, a key piece of legislation—the Law of Return, adopted in 1950—was enacted to grant automatic Israeli citizenship to Jewish immigrants from throughout the diaspora. "Every Jew," it stated, "has the right to come to this country as an *oleh* (immigrant)." But whom did the state regard as a Jew? Although the issue was of key importance, it was so contentious that the legislature, the Knesset, chose to avoid addressing it at all.

Especially in secular circles, there were many who held that the new conditions of Jewish life in the State of Israel rendered rabbinic criteria no longer applicable for determining who was a Jew. Ben-Gurion, whose *mamlakhti* (statist) ideology was widely shared by secular Zionists, put it this way: "Here [in Israel] we are not a minority under pressure of a foreign culture, and there is no fear of assimilation of Jews among non-Jews. While abroad mixed marriages are one of the decisive factors in the total assimilation and in the abandonment of Judaism, the couples in mixed marriages arriving here, especially from Eastern Europe, actually fuse completely with the Jewish people." The conditions of exile had thus been reversed, so that the dominant dynamic was now one of assimilation of the Gentile, not the Jew. In Ben-Gurion's ethnonational conception of Jewishness, the Gentile partner would blend into Israeli Jewish society by a natural process, much as had occurred in biblical times. Indeed, the biblical model was very much present in Ben-Gurion's mind. Moses, he pointed out, had married a Midianite woman who became an Israelite without the intercession of three rabbis. And there was, of course, another factor: The state needed people, and it should allow them to come.[1]

His firmly held convictions notwithstanding, Ben-Gurion could not do without support from the religious parties. In 1958 the secularist head of the Interior Ministry sparked a crisis when he issued instructions that anyone could declare him- or herself a Jew and be officially registered as such. In response, the National Religious Party threatened to withdraw from the government. The issue had great practical importance, given the many mixed couples arriving from Europe. To resolve the crisis, Ben-Gurion turned to fifty-one Jewish intellectuals, asking them to offer their opinion as to "how to register the 'religion' and 'nationhood' of the children of mixed marriages when the father is Jewish and the mother is not Jewish and has not converted" and the parents wanted their child registered as a Jew by religion. Most of the respondents—among them, secular Jews—favored the use of traditional rabbinic criteria, holding that children with non-Jewish mothers needed to undergo *giyyur* to be registered as Jews. As a pragmatic matter, Ben-Gurion and the Ministry of the Interior accepted this view, although it was not written into law.

Despite his generally welcoming attitude to Jewish immigrants of all stripes, Ben-Gurion was firmly opposed to granting citizenship to Jews who had converted "out." Indifferent to halakhic dicta that held Jewishness to be indelible, he believed that a Jew who underwent baptism became, in effect, a Gentile. This position became government policy. When in 1958 the Polish-born baptized Jew Oswald Rufeisen (better known as "Brother Daniel") sought Israeli citizenship under the Law of Return, the government refused to register him as a Jew. The case was appealed to the Supreme Court, which in 1962 ruled against Rufeisen. Justice Zvi Berenson explained that by converting to Christianity Rufeisen had "disassociated himself from the religion, the people, and the community of Israel"; he concurred with Ben-Gurion that a person "cannot be both Jewish and Christian."[2]

The Brother Daniel case implied that being a Jew entailed something more than Jewish ancestry. But what exactly? No one disputed that secular Jews were Jews in every respect. Could a non-believing Gentile, then, become a non-believing Jew? In 1970 the Benjamin Shalit case provoked a public crisis on just such a question. Immigrants, like all Israelis, were registered in the population registry under two categories: "nationality" and "religion." The Israeli Supreme Court had ruled that Shalit, an Israeli Jew married to a non-Jewish immigrant, could register his children in just the way that he proposed—as Jewish by nationality and as "having no religion."[3] The ruling provoked a storm of criticism because it seemed to imply that Jewish identity was a subjective, personal matter.

To provide some clarity, the Knesset stepped in, amending the Law of Return in 1970. In effect, it formalized the standard that had been adopted more than a decade earlier, stipulating that "for the purposes of this Law, 'Jew' means a person who was born of a Jewish mother or has become converted to Judaism and who is not a member of another religion." The wording of the amendment was important. Implicit was the Knesset's rejection of demands that conversion be performed according to Orthodox halakha. A person who underwent a Reform conversion would by implication be eligible for citizenship. The amendment did not stop there. It opened the way for the naturalization of non-Jewish, unconverted family members of Jews. These included spouses, children of non-Jewish mothers and their children, and spouses of such children and grandchildren. These persons would have the full rights of citizens. However, unless they converted, they would not be registered as Jews. At the time, this provision did not have major consequences.

The ambiguity of the 1970 amendment, which said nothing about *whose* conversions would be accepted for purposes of the Law of Return, was removed in 1986. In that year Shoshanna Miller, a new immigrant who had converted to Judaism in the United States, challenged the Interior Ministry for issuing her an Israeli ID card that, although identifying her as a Jew, added the qualifier "convert." The label appeared to cast doubt on the validity of her Reform conversion. The Supreme Court ruled that the ministry was not authorized to add such a label on an ID card.

Yet the Supreme Court recognized the need for *some* standard by which it could rule conversions valid or invalid for the purposes of the Law of Return. Several years later it adopted one: To be registered as Jews, converts to Judaism would need to supply documentation from a "recognized community outside of Israel." The communities thus recognized were the three major diaspora streams—Orthodox, Conservative, and Reform. However, Conservative and Reform conversions were accepted in this way only if performed "outside of Israel." In Israel itself, where the status quo arrangement was in force, only conversions performed under the auspices of Orthodox religious courts were recognized by the state.[4]

By the 1970s public pressure was growing in Israel to create a less stringent path to conversion. In the wake of the Six-Day War in 1967, increasing numbers of non-Jewish volunteers were arriving on kibbutzim, marrying kibbutz members and staying. Non-Jewish spouses were also arriving among the trickle of Jewish immigrants from the Soviet Union. When these immigrants turned to the rabbinic courts for conversion, they were routinely rejected because it was clearly not their intention to conduct their lives according to halakha.

The chief architect of an alternative path was the independent-minded Shlomo Goren, Chief Ashkenazi rabbi from 1972 to 1983. While head of the military rabbinate in the 1960s, Goren had already established a streamlined conversion process for soldiers (mainly the children of immigrants with non-Jewish mothers).[5] As chief rabbi, he circumvented the rabbinic courts by establishing a state conversion authority with rabbis appointed by him to serve in special conversion courts. To prepare potential converts he instituted conversion courses that were conducted under the aegis not of the rabbinate but of government ministries.

Goren's thinking and activity around conversion had a radically new thrust. In contrast to ultra-Orthodox and more cautious Religious Zionist rabbis, Goren believed that the realities of the new Jewish state necessitated an explicit rethinking of the requirements for (and indeed the meaning of) conversion. It was the role of the state, he believed, to actively support and encourage the conversion of non-Jewish immigrants. From his Zionist perspective, the Jewish people in Israel were being molded anew by the state and its institutions, and the rabbinic establishment needed to recognize its obligation not just to the religious sector but also to the entire Jewish people.

Goren's highly dichotomized vision of Jewish life—one in which diaspora existence was fundamentally different from existence in the Jewish state—deeply informed his thinking about conversion. Somewhat in the vein of Ben-Gurion, he believed that the great majority of those who were presenting themselves for conversion in Israel, though far from religiously motivated, would in time be shaped by their Jewish environment. He drew on classical sources to make his point. The sages of the Babylonian Talmud, he maintained, inhabited a diasporic reality that inhibited the convert's integration into Jewish life, and for this reason they adopted a negative attitude to conversion. In contrast, the Jerusalem Talmud sages, who were anchored in Eretz Israel where conditions favored the convert's integration, embraced a positive attitude—an example, he held, that the rabbinic leadership of the State of Israel should follow.[6]

By shifting the focus from the inner motivations of converts to the power of the environment to condition them, Goren placed national and sociological considerations squarely within the orbit of halakhic reasoning about *giyyur.* It is interesting in this respect that on several occasions he compared the non-Jews among Israel's immigrant population to the Idumeans, a foreign ethnic group living in a Jewish polity whom the Hasmoneans converted en masse as a matter of national interest. He was not, to be sure, recommending forced conversion. But even the Idumeans, he maintained, eventually became fully Jewish.[7] This is not to say that Goren lacked apprehension about his approach. Indeed, his misgivings led him to adopt an extraordinary and unprecedented policy: Aware that converts under the state-managed program would most likely not be religiously observant after their *giyyur,* he made their status conditional on their continued residence in Israel (a practice that ended with his tenure).[8]

For a while after Goren stepped down as chief rabbi in 1983, it looked as if his initiative had run its course. The power of the ultra-Orthodox (or *haredim*), who bitterly opposed what they regarded as invalid conversions, was growing. An influential wing of the National Religious camp (known by the acronym *hardal*) moved closer in its religious outlook to the *haredim*. From 1993 onward, the Chief Rabbinate reflected an essentially *haredi* outlook, one that was intolerant of the life choices of Israelis who lived outside its orbit. In keeping with this outlook, it required a detailed commitment to halakhic observance from potential converts, of a kind that had little precedent in Jewish law. The roster of rabbis willing to perform conversions under the state conversion authority shrank, conversion courses were terminated, and ministerial budgets for dealing with conversion were cut.[9] Yet the number of non-Jewish immigrants was only growing. In 1989, with the fall of the Soviet Union, the floodgates opened. According to the Ministry of Absorption, between 1990 and 2001 more than 200,000 immigrants from the Former Soviet Union (FSU) were registered as non-Jews at the Interior Ministry, a number that grew substantially in subsequent years.[10]

By far the most pressing issues today in the realm of conversion in Israel concern this population. As of this writing, a half-million or so Israeli citizens are registered in the population registry as non-Jews, yet they live as Jews in Israeli society and are, to use a phrase adopted by scholars, "sociological Jews."[11] Their anomalous status prevents them from officially marrying a Jew in Israel, because Jewish marriages are in the hands of the Chief Rabbinate's courts and civil marriage is not an option. The state conversion authority in Israel has particularly targeted female FSU immigrants with messages encouraging conversion, because as women they will determine halakhically the identity of their children.[12] This may explain in part why about 80 percent of immigrants from the FSU who have undergone conversion are women.[13] Of course, these women may themselves be motivated to undergo the conversion process because they are the ones who will determine their children's Jewish identity, while their male counterparts feel no such responsibility.[14]

The growing number of immigrants from the FSU, on the one hand, and the increasingly stringent requirements for accepting conversions under *haredi*-controlled regional religious courts, on the other, led to a crisis in 1995. Reform and Conservative leaders in Israel, indignant at the Chief Rabbinate's disrespect toward them and its indifference to their concerns about the handling of conversion, added to the pressure to find a solution. As a result, the government appointed the Ne'eman Commission in 1997. Its recommendation that a new state conversion authority be established and administered by the Prime Minister's Office was implemented. There was an unsuccessful attempt to create a joint instruction program as part of this initiative in which teachers from the Reform, Conservative, and Orthodox camps would all participate. In practice, teachers from the Religious Zionist wing of Orthodoxy provide instruction. The actual ritual conversions are conducted by *haredi*-leaning Orthodox religious courts. Since 2001 the program, renamed Nativ, has extended its activity to the army, preparing non-Jewish soldiers for conversion.[15]

Although the rabbinic courts that perform these conversions are part of the state bureaucracy, the rabbinic judges who officiate do not share the broadly based national values that the state is intended to embody. From a Zionist point of view, the conversion of as many as possible is, in the words of Labor MK Ofir Pines, "a national interest" and serves the "collective desire of all—religious and secular, Orthodox and non-Orthodox—to preserve and strengthen the Jewish majority in the State of Israel."[16] The instructors in the state conversion program whose task is to prepare candidates for conversion tend to share this view, and their extended contact with the candidates instills realism about the range of their motivations.[17] Yet most of the rabbinic judges on the state conversion courts come from the *haredi* orbit and do not recognize the national interest as a legitimate factor in authorizing conversions. Their hostility toward the secular world renders them poorly suited to grasping the perspective of immigrants from the FSU who have been conditioned from early childhood to a secular existence. That presumably contributes to the program's limited effectiveness given the enormous pool of halakhic non-Jews it was designed to reach: It conducts only around one thousand conversions per year.[18]

The state conversion authority is not, however, the only body performing conversions in Israel, even though it is the only one whose conversions are automatically recognized by the Interior Ministry. Both the Reform and Conservative movements, which have put down roots in Israel, have conversion programs reflecting their distinct sensibilities and expectations for observance. (In 2023, after years of deliberation, Israel's High Court ruled that non-Orthodox conversions performed in Israel are valid for the purposes of the Law of Return.) The nonprofit Religious Zionist organization Itim offers a program specifically aimed at secular Israelis who are not halakhically Jewish, providing conversions by an Orthodox *beit din*. The program aims to make the halakhic tradition accessible in the hope that its converts will adopt, in the words of its director, a "Jewish lifestyle."[19] Nongovernmental *haredi* conversion courts also operate outside the purview of the state conversion authority.

Yet despite the various efforts to effectuate their *giyyur*, most of the "sociological Jews" with FSU origins have resisted any form of conversion, despite concerted efforts to ease the process.[20] This is in part because they consider themselves already Jewish and in part because they plan to live as secular Jews and are not willing to pretend otherwise. According to a survey conducted in 2003 among *olim* from the FSU who were registered as non-Jews, 75 percent had no intention of converting to Judaism.[21] They can easily circumvent the restrictions this status entails. They cannot marry Jews officially in Israel, but they can go abroad to wed—and often do so in nearby Cyprus. Some form households without marrying. In their everyday lives, they have "become" Jews. They live like other secular Israelis, albeit outside the classic rabbinic parameters of Jewish belonging. And they do so in unprecedented numbers.

Most Israelis are content to have such persons as neighbors and fellow workers and see them as integrated members of Israel's Jewish sector. Yet by their own admission they would not want them as spouses for their children.[22] In this as in other matters, Israeli Jews tend to harbor a basic respect for traditional criteria for determining Jewishness. Thus, although in recent years some groups have floated proposals for creating a path to joining the Jewish people on secular, ethnocultural terms, they have garnered little public support or interest.[23]

In recent years, concern has grown about the anomalous phenomenon of the retroactive nullification of Orthodox conversions, usually on grounds that the convert has not been leading a halakhically observant life.[24] A particularly bitter controversy broke out in 2008 when the presiding rabbi on the religious appellate court, Avraham Sherman, nullified thousands of conversions overseen by the Religious Zionist rabbi Haim Druckman. This ruling represented, in the words of one scholar, "nothing less than an outright campaign by ultra-Orthodox rabbis against the authority of Orthodox Zionist rabbis to perform halakhic conversions."[25] Caught in the middle were the converts involved, whose status and sense of security were suddenly undermined. Although Sherman's ruling was eventually overturned, the episode further deepened the turmoil around issues of conversion at a time when many Israelis resent an increasingly *haredi* religious establishment—one they feel is indifferent to the social, cultural, and human realities of their everyday lives.

Meanwhile, the population of Israelis who regard themselves as Jews but whose formal personal status is that of Gentiles continues to grow. The unwieldy arrangement that has evolved breeds a good deal of cynicism and personal distress and deepens the fault lines in Israeli society. Many regard the current situation as unsustainable. A solution, however, remains elusive.

8 United States

In the post-war Jewish diaspora, the conversation around conversion has been subject to a very different constellation of factors—political, cultural, and demographic—than in Israel. Given the confines of this book, I focus on American Jewry, the largest and most thoroughly studied diaspora population.[1] Although in Israel the state (and the Orthodox religious authority it empowers) ultimately determined the religious status of its citizens and set the terms for conversion for those who were not halakhically Jewish, in the United States the state was, as a matter of principle, indifferent to the religious status of its citizens. And whereas in Israel the Jewish sector was demographically dominant, with a prevailing Zionist vision that encouraged the perpetuation and development of Jewish life, in the United States Jews were a small but integrated minority, one that tended to share widespread ideals of multiculturalism and diversity.

A survey carried out in 1953 found that 94 percent of conversions in the United States were related to marriage—certainly a reflection not only of secularizing and assimilatory trends but also of a striking new openness to Judaism among American Gentiles. As in the previous century, the great majority of converts were women: The same 1953 survey found a ratio of more than four female converts to every male.[2] This striking discrepancy has not essentially changed over time. A survey of 439 Orthodox conversions conducted in the United States in 2015 revealed that 78 percent of the converts were women.[3] Scholars have not adequately addressed the reasons for this imbalance, which remains largely a matter of speculation. The sheer number of converts to Judaism in the postwar period was unprecedented. Equally unprecedented, however—and a source of deep anxiety—was the fact that more than four of five mixed couples lived secular lives and saw no need for either spouse to convert.[4]

Awareness of a steep rise in the number of intermarriages in postwar America came with the publication in 1971 of a National Jewish Population Study that showed the rate among Jews to be a shocking 32 percent. (It has since risen.) Jewish leaders quickly identified the trend as a threat to Jewish survival. In such an environment the potential conversion of non-Jewish spouses ceased to be a private matter between marriage partners and became a very public issue, fundamental to Jewish communal policymaking. There was a certain paradox in this reaction. High intermarriage rates reflected the dominant modern ideal of marriage as a romantic relationship between two individuals, unaffected by the pressures that family and community had historically exerted. Yet it was precisely in the liberal sectors of Jewish society where this ideal was most valued that communities felt compelled to take action to sway couples in mixed marriages to consider the conversion of the non-Jewish spouse. The initiatives these communities accordingly undertook were known as "outreach"—a term that softened what might certainly be regarded as a form of proselytization.

Concern over intermarriage provided the motivation for major sociological studies of conversion in postwar America. Steven Huberman's 1979 study of Reform conversions, *New Jews: The Dynamics of Religious Conversion*, was unapologetically subtitled *A Summary Report of the Intermarriage and Conversion Project*. Similarly, Egon Mayer and Amy Avgar published a study in 1987 titled *Conversion Among the Intermarried: Choosing to Become Jewish*.[5] Sylvia Barack Fishman's 2006 analysis, *Choosing Jewish: Conversations About Conversion*, was motivated by the same sense of urgency. "Conversion into Judaism," she wrote, "is a topic of intense interest in the American Jewish community today because more than one-third of American Jews are married to non-Jews, and close to half of recent 'Jewish' marriages are mixed marriages between persons of Jewish and non-Jewish descent."[6]

These sociological studies and others, supported by the American Jewish Committee and other Jewish organizations, offer a window into patterns of conversion among intermarried couples and into a distinctly American style of discourse around conversion. The contrast with the classic rabbinic model, in which potential converts came forward on their own initiative and a rabbinic court responded by providing halakhic instruction and rendering a verdict, is striking. What transpired in the conversions reported in these studies was more akin to a collaborative project—one in which non-Jewish spouses or romantic partners (mostly women) participated in ongoing conversations and interactions with their Jewish spouses or partners, their in-laws, their parents, and the rabbis who in a pastoral mode accompanied them along the way. Power relations were strikingly altered under these circumstances and reflected not only the absence of coercive communal controls but also the internalization of American democratic sensibilities, as well as the realities of a religious marketplace where people were free to seek out supportive clergy.[7] A program of study for potential converts was, of course, prescribed—one in which the Jewish partner ideally participated and that introduced the couple to Jewish practices, beliefs, and values. But the potential convert was essentially entrusted with the decision whether to convert, and the act of *giyyur* was less a rite marking a dramatic break than the natural outcome of a complex working out of a new identity and way of life.

The Conservative movement and the various Orthodox streams have consistently resisted proselytization and have continued to require from converts a commitment to their respective halakhic standards, at least in principle. From their vantage point, the most problematic aspect of *giyyur* in the postwar period has been the creation outside the Orthodox orbit of a population of converts (and descendants of female converts) who are not, in their view, Jews at all. When such persons have chosen to join Conservative or Orthodox congregations, they have been required to undergo a second or even third conversion. However distressing such reconversion may be for those concerned, it has offered a solution to the problem on a case-by-case basis. But concern persists about the great majority of non-Orthodox converts who do not take this step and thus constitute a population whose Jewish status is insecure and contested.

Differences among Orthodox, Conservative, and Reform streams over the validity of non-Orthodox conversions had already emerged in the nineteenth century, as we saw. But the increasing numbers of those conversions heightened the concern. The assumption that Jews, despite their dispersion, constitute a single ethnoreligious body is profoundly rooted in Jewish tradition. It is reflected in liturgy, halakhic discourse, Jewish philosophical thought, and Jewish organizational life. With few exceptions, unity has been maintained over the centuries; cases of *giyyur* did not pose a challenge, because one *beit din*'s conversion was universally accepted by others. The new situation in the United States, where rabbinic authority was fragmented, assimilation and intermarriage were widespread, and conversions were relatively common, raised the troubling possibility of an eventual split. Particularly high rates of female conversion heightened the potential problem, given that all the descendants of a woman whose conversion was not recognized would be regarded as Gentiles. The title of a 1986 essay written by the liberal Orthodox rabbi Irving Greenberg—"Will There Be One Jewish People by the Year 2000?"—was emblematic of the situation.

The problem was sufficiently alarming that several Jewish leaders were prompted to ask whether it might be possible to institute a process of *giyyur* that would be accepted by all elements of the Jewish community. There were considerable obstacles to doing so. First, the conversion process entailed instruction in the essentials of the Jewish tradition, but there was disagreement about what those were. The Reform movement placed little emphasis on the learning of Hebrew, and although it valued certain Jewish customs, it focused strongly on the universal moral ideals of Jewish tradition. The Conservative movement respected the rabbinic tradition but adhered to its own halakha and, among other differences, manifested a greater commitment than the Orthodox to gender equality. The Orthodox stream made relatively few concessions to modern liberal values, placing greater weight on the ethos reflected in classical texts; it sought to inculcate commitment to a halakhically governed way of life that stood at variance with the norms of US society. It was not clear how a coherent curriculum could be devised that would satisfy all sides. It is true that since the 1970s the Reform movement had modified its once-radical repudiation of particularistic ritual, actively encouraging Sabbath and Jewish dietary practices and integrating more Hebrew into the liturgy. Still, a yawning gap separated the Reform movement's cautious incorporation of certain ritual practices and the extensive obligations that Orthodoxy imposed.

Second, attitudes about the very desirability of conversion differed. Reform leaders saw the primary function of conversion as fighting defections from Jewish communal life; as such they viewed not only conversion but also the active proselytization of non-Jewish spouses as having intrinsic value. Orthodox rabbis, in contrast, tended to view conversion as a privilege, one that was granted only to highly motivated persons with a sincere commitment to an Orthodox way of life. Consistent with their respective attitudes, the different streams greeted candidates for conversion with varied degrees of openness. To complicate matters further, those Orthodox leaders who felt impelled to cooperate with the non-Orthodox to find a solution faced intense pressure from the right wing of their camp to abstain from doing so.

Yet genuine anxiety over the possibility that the fundamental ethnoreligious bond uniting Jews might be broken drove an effort to try to find common ground. An initial effort in the 1950s was abandoned when negotiations to create a joint Orthodox and Conservative national *beit din* broke down. Then, in 1978, overcoming the various challenges in a rare show of goodwill, a joint Traditional/Orthodox, Conservative, and Reform *beit din* for conversion was established in Denver.[8] A board comprising rabbis from all three streams established a single educational program for conversion candidates. The rabbis rotated as instructors, presenting their own perspectives while trying to emphasize common elements. On completion of the course, candidates were examined by the board. If deemed ready for conversion, they were turned over to a Traditional/Orthodox *beit din* for ritual conversion, including circumcision or *hatafat dam* for males, immersion, and a general declaration of *kabbalat ha-mitzvot* ("acceptance of commandments," an act that was taken seriously but without severe demands). Although during their preparation candidates might meet with rabbis from one or another stream, they were not labeled "Reform," "Conservative," or "Orthodox" converts: They were all granted the essential status of born Jews.

In the six years of the Denver program's existence, the joint *beit din* performed some 750 conversions. The program was, however, short-lived. It was dissolved in 1983 when the Reform movement, breaking sharply with traditional notions of Jewish identity, issued a resolution recognizing patrilineal Jewish descent, to the dismay of both Conservative and Orthodox parties. Adding to the problem was the Reform movement's launching of a project in Denver to encourage the conversion of Gentile spouses, which threatened to turn the rabbinic judges on the joint *beit din* into participants in Reform proselytization efforts.[9]

If there was little chance for such a project to succeed after the Reform movement's resolution in 1983, chances for cooperation have only dimmed with time. The different streams in American Jewish life have pursued largely independent trajectories in handling conversion, shaped by both internal exigencies and external pressures. In recent years, the Chief Rabbinate in Israel, reflecting its increasingly *haredi* stance, has exerted its influence over diaspora Orthodoxy, recognizing as legitimate for marriage in Israel only those diaspora conversions performed by Orthodox rabbinical courts that have its approval.

At its most extreme, Orthodox halakhic reasoning has led to the conclusion that, in the conditions of modern life, *giyyur* is so likely to be disingenuous that it should be disallowed altogether. Such a view has led to a blanket prohibition on conversion within an entire American community. The origins of this ban were in the ruling of a Buenos Aires rabbi in 1927 prohibiting rabbis in the tight-knit Aleppo (Syrian) community of Argentina from performing conversions.[10] Historically such a ban was unprecedented. It was precipitated by the perception that conversions were facilitating marriages "out" and thus contributing to the shocking erosion of traditional values that immigrant rabbis encountered in Argentina. In 1935 a similar ban was issued by the *beit din* of the Syrian community in Brooklyn. It prohibited marriages to non-Jews and declared conversions "fictitious and valueless." There is disagreement as to just how effective that ban was in practice. Couples who defied the ban, however, were barred from participation in communal life, and their children were not permitted to marry within the community. (Not surprisingly, many left.) The ban was reaffirmed several times, most recently in 2006, and its scope was extended to include Syrian communities elsewhere in the New York metropolitan area, as well as in Florida.[11]

This prohibition has meant, among other things, that the Syrian Jewish community in the United States has remained ethnically homogeneous. This sets it apart from the trend in American Jewish communities more generally, where conversion is one of the factors contributing to increased racial and ethnic heterogeneity. The growing number of African American Jews—that is, members of Jewish communities (not to be confused with Black Israelites, who do not identify with historic Judaism)—and of persons who identify as both Black and Jewish has challenged old assumptions about the ethnic character of US Jewry. According to a scholar who has conducted interviews with Black converts, these Jews tend to associate Christianity, the faith in which they were raised, with the masters who imposed that religion on their ancestors; they can identify more easily with the religion of the Israelites who escaped from Egyptian bondage. In any case, Black Jews who have undergone conversion (or who are children of biracial marriages in which a parent has converted) are members of all the major streams of American Jewish life.[12]

In the late twentieth and early twenty-first centuries, many young Americans have gravitated to movements with roots in the 1960s counterculture that reflect dissatisfaction with traditional frameworks of organized religion. These new forms of spirituality draw on elements of Eastern and other religious traditions, integrating them with New Age concepts and practices. The more radical Jewish expressions of this trend—most notably, the Kabbalah Centre in Los Angeles, made famous in the 1990s by Madonna—are indifferent to established boundaries and codes, including the rabbinic gatekeeping associated with conversion. They welcome whoever participates, Jew or non-Jew. Their focus on psychic healing and personal transformation represents a sharp departure from the communal, ethnoreligious foundations of historic Judaism. They provide commitment-free, easily accessible forms of spirituality that "spiritual shoppers" can piece together with beliefs and practices from other sources. What they offer, as one scholar wryly described it, is "consumable religion tailored to the self-focused lifestyle of the postmodern seeker."[13] In these respects they are part of a more general American phenomenon.[14]

Jewish Renewal and neo-Hassidism share some of the hallmarks of these movements. But they are decidedly Jewish, even if they have done away with traditional structures of Jewish communal learning and authority. Although their communities are small, they reflect a distinctive Jewish response to the social and ideological landscape of the contemporary United States. Their democratized, inclusive, accessible expressions of Jewish spirituality attract young people alienated by mainstream synagogue culture, as well as spiritual seekers from other backgrounds. For them, the rabbinic boundary maintenance underlying the practice of *giyyur* seems irrelevant to modern existence, with its multiethnic populations and its pluralistic and universalistic orientation. Zalman Schachter-Shalomi, one of the founders of Jewish Renewal, encouraged the acceptance into the Jewish community of non-Jews who "feel guided to be *also* Jewish"—who do not want to take on an exclusively Jewish identity but rather want to construct and celebrate a multiform one. Such persons would not be halakhic converts but rather modern-day exemplars, in his view, of the biblical *ger toshav*.[15] The radically pluralistic ideology of Jewish Renewal challenges, among other things, the classic model according to which belonging to a religion means not belonging to any other and conversion entails the rejection of a former religious affiliation (or former religious indifference).[16]

To some degree, the embrace by Jewish Renewal of the values of diversity, inclusiveness, and egalitarianism has had echoes in inherently more conservative mainstream communities. This is unsurprising given the broad appeal of these themes in contemporary American public life. In a notable statement in

2019, the president of the Union for Reform Judaism, concerned by high rates of intermarriage and the need to compete in the US religious marketplace, called on his movement to welcome into the community Americans who were "Jewishly adjacent"—that is, who would qualify to become Israeli citizens under the Law of Return by virtue of their relationship to acknowledged Jews, despite not being Jewish by halakhic definitions. He emphasized the need to allow such persons a collaborative role in creating community, "instead of asking them to [accept] the way we have always done it." This was a striking departure from traditional conceptualizations of how an outsider might enter the Jewish community, which took for granted a convert's acceptance of norms established by communal leadership.[17]

In recent decades, as the internet and social media have transformed the way culture is transmitted and have addressed every imaginable need, Jewish-Renewal-style spirituality has proved readily transferrable to the new platforms. Online conversion courses are now a click away. Darshan Yeshiva, operating from Atlanta, boasts that it has among its educators "Reform, Conservative, Jewish Renewal, Secular Humanistic and Post-Denominational rabbis" and offers differently priced options.[18] The online organization Sim Shalom informs conversion candidates that after completing an online study program, which they can do "in just a few short months," they will have an online meeting with a *beit din*, after which they will receive "an emailed certificate of conversion, affirming your complete integration into the Jewish faith."[19] Another such website invites prospective converts to Judaism to "customize your [conversion] ceremony."[20] In this new commodified conceptualization, *giyyur* has become a product available in several models; it reflects an American popular culture in which customer satisfaction is a priority and "identity" can be shed or acquired effortlessly.

In the first decades of the twenty-first century, at least in some quarters, defining oneself Jewishly has become closely associated not only with what one chooses to be or what a religious authority declares one to be but also with what one's DNA says one is. It is now possible to undergo a personal "conversion" of sorts after the discovery or affirmation of Jewish ancestry through genetic testing—a phenomenon that has been duly recognized by the marketers of genetic tests. Indeed, the wide availability of and interest in such testing have contributed to what has been called the "biologization" of Jewish identity, with its inherent echoes of racial discourse and its challenge to the most fundamental assumption underlying the process of *giyyur*.[21]

In conclusion, in an environment characterized by so much variation and unclarity as to what it means to be a Jew, there can be no consensus about what it means to *become* a Jew. Within the three streams of mainstream American Jewish life there are disagreements over the validity of certain conversions, over the Jewish status of children of mixed marriages when the father is a Jew, and over what commitments should be required of converts—all of which have made consensus on conversion elusive. Yet there is fundamental agreement about the nature of Judaism as a distinctive historic tradition that fuses peoplehood and religion. There is also agreement about the basic nature of conversion as a process that requires study, as well as commitment to and participation in established forms of communal institutional life. This basic conception has in recent decades been challenged by forms of Jewish spirituality that have an antiestablishment if not openly subversive thrust. By stressing private, subjective, self-focused ways of experiencing Jewishness, these movements have cast aside both the ethnic component of Jewishness and the very notion of rabbinic authority. However, they remain marginal demographically and have little presence in the public arena, and it is not clear how influential or enduring they will be.

9 "Emerging Jews"

Over the centuries Jewish tradition has represented Jew and Gentile as standing in binary opposition: A person was either one or the other. This was consistent with a view of the Jewish world itself as constituted of well-bounded Jewish communities with a continuous history dating back to time immemorial. There were exceptions—the conversos of the Iberian world were a striking one—but they were few. Even in the modern period, when the boundaries separating Jew and Gentile blurred throughout much of the diaspora, a person's Jewish identity continued to imply descent from one or another of the established Jewish ethnocultural communities. The "imagined community" of world Jewry was well demarcated and securely rooted in history.

With the establishment of the State of Israel, the commitment of Israel's leaders to absorbing as many immigrants as possible, accompanied by a romanticized view of the power of the Land of Israel to transform *galus* Jews (Jews of the exile), encouraged a more expansive, outward-looking view of the Jewish world. To recruit *olim*, Zionist emissaries traveled to communities that had long been cut off from contact with the great centers of Jewish life. Their travels brought attention to small populations scattered across the globe, including some whose claims to Jewish origins were doubtful. Itzhak Ben-Zvi, ethnologist, Labor Zionist, and the second president of Israel, gave enthusiastic if paternalistic and heavily Zionist expression to a new, capacious vision of the Jewish people, one that included "forgotten Jews" and celebrated their resettlement in Israel.[1]

A different interest in "forgotten Jews" also developed in the late twentieth century. Scholars in the emerging field of identity studies, fascinated by groups with complex, ambiguous identities and inspired by a postmodern interest in the marginalized and suppressed, have been drawn to Jews at the fringes. Their studies, often relying heavily on oral traditions, family narratives, and personal memories, tend to confer validation on subjective, popular forms of Jewish identity. Without documented genealogical records, however, the status of such groups has often been uncertain—not only from a rabbinic perspective but also in popular Jewish perception.

In some cases, like that of the Jews of Mashhad in Iran (whose origins were discussed in chapter 6), doubts were resolved rather easily. The Mashhadi Jews had been forcibly converted to Islam in 1839, but as accounts of foreign visitors attested, the converts and their descendants, although behaving outwardly as Muslims, conducted their lives as Jews, often with the tacit consent of Iranian authorities. They adhered to basic Jewish traditions, married among themselves, and maintained contact to some degree with the wider Jewish world. When in 1946 a Jewish Agency official pressed for the immigration of about a thousand of the Mashhadi Jews to Palestine, the two chief rabbis of Israel were consulted about their religious status. Yitzhak Herzog, the Ashkenazi chief rabbi, raised questions about possible intermarriage among them but did not question the Jewish status of most members of the community. His Sephardi counterpart, Benzion Uziel, flatly declared the entire population to be "pure Jews." Immigration proceeded without objection, and the Jewish status of the tight-knit communities that the Mashhadi emigres built in Israel and elsewhere (mainly New York) has been unquestioned.[2]

Better known, thanks to Frédéric Brenner's 1991 film *The Last Marranos* and regular heritage tourism visits, are the descendants of crypto-Jews in Belmonte and other rural villages in the Trás-os-Montes region of Portugal who were discovered by the Polish-born Jewish mining engineer Samuel Schwarz in 1917. Schwarz's 1925 work *Os cristãos novos em Portugal no século XX* (The New Christians of Portugal in the Twentieth Century) described the practices of the Belmonte community and sparked the interest of the international Jewish community. Initial efforts at intervention were short-lived, however, and during the repressive Salazar regime, from 1926 to 1974, the Belmonte crypto-Jews maintained a low profile. It has only been since the 1980s that members of the Belmonte community have actively sought contact with the outside Jewish world. The Jewish Agency sent an Orthodox rabbi to provide instruction, and the Belmonte community began to undergo a transformation, one that was given impetus by the influx into their town of scholars, journalists, and tourists. Although the community undoubtedly had crypto-Jewish origins, its members could not prove unbroken Jewish descent. To be accepted fully as Jews, in the 1990s about half the community—about a hundred Jews—underwent Orthodox conversion.[3]

In distinct contrast to the Mashhadi Jews and the Belmonte crypto-Jews, which had documentable roots in Jewish historical experience, are various groups about whom claims have been made of Jewish origins (sometimes drawing on DNA studies).[4] Although they have elicited attention from ethnographers and journalists, they cannot be dealt with in this slim volume, especially because issues of conversion are secondary, for different reasons in each case. Among these groups are members of the Igbo of Nigeria and of the Lemba of South Africa[5]; the self-described *anusim* and *Marranos* of Latin America, the American Southwest, Portugal, and Spain[6]; and the Black Israelites in the United States and Israel, whose religio-racial self-understandings have entailed a rejection of "white" Jewish authenticity (and thus of any reason to undergo rabbinic conversion).[7] I focus on a few groups whose aspirations have dovetailed with and been supported (and shaped) by outside Zionist and Orthodox Jewish agents, promoting their immigration to Israel and participation in conversion programs.

The best-known case, and the one with the greatest demographic impact, is that of the Ethiopian Beta Israel (and, more recently, the Falashmura).[8] Traditions about the existence of Jews living "beyond the rivers of Cush" go back to Eldad ha-Dani in the ninth century. These Jews entered rabbinic discussion in the sixteenth century, when the Spanish exile and rabbinic scholar David ibn Zimra (known by the acronym "Radbaz") ruled on two cases involving Jews in Egypt from "the land of Cush" whose knowledge of Judaism came entirely from Scripture. Radbaz ruled that these Jews were "without a doubt from the tribe of Dan." It was thus a commandment to redeem (rather than simply purchase) a slave from this population. Although Radbaz noted the questionability of these Jews' lineage, given their nonrabbinic practices of marriage and divorce, he concluded that they should be allowed to marry other Jews once they accepted rabbinic Judaism.[9]

Foreign awareness of this population subsequently disappeared and was renewed only in the mid-nineteenth century when Protestant missionaries discovered and began evangelizing them.[10] The missionaries' reports about the possible Jewish origins of a group they were missionizing aroused the concern of European Jewish leaders. Most importantly, publicity around them led to the lifelong campaign of the Polish-born French Jew Jacques Faitlovitch to "regenerate" what he passionately believed to be a Jewish population. This is not the place to discuss why Faitlovitch and other foreign Jews believed the Beta Israel (or "Falashas," as they were pejoratively known by outsiders) had Jewish origins. Suffice it to say that belief in those origins became the justification for a succession of programs aimed to educate the group in modern cultural practices and rabbinic Judaism. Up to World War II, European and American Jewish organizations funded and conducted these efforts. In the postwar period, the initiative passed to the Jewish Agency and other Israeli institutions.[11]

Over the course of several generations, these efforts brought about a transformation, however uneven, of the cultural, religious, and identitarian outlook of the Beta Israel—one that certainly could be considered a collective conversion. The motivations behind the Ethiopians' responsiveness varied and included aspirations for a better material life, greater security, and broader horizons. For their part, the Jews who sponsored the efforts understood the need to preserve aspects of traditional Beta Israel religious culture. A key aspect of the project from the Israeli perspective involved preparing these Jews (as they now regarded themselves and were regarded by others) for mass immigration to Israel. In 1973 Chief Rabbi Ovadiah Yosef ruled that the Ethiopian Jews were fully Jews, echoing Radbaz in declaring them to be descendants of the tribe of Dan. This set the stage for their immigration to Israel under the

Law of Return. Between 1977 and 1993, in a complex and much-publicized operation, the Israeli government organized the airlift to Israel of virtually all the Beta Israel, many of whom had endured terrible suffering fleeing famine in Ethiopia before arriving in refugee camps in Sudan.[12]

Initially, the immigrants were not registered as Jews by the Ministry of the Interior unless they underwent a modified form of conversion to remove doubt (*giyyur le-humra*).[13] A ruling of the High Court in 1984 led to the removal of this requirement for the purpose of registration. Yet, even though the Ethiopian immigrants were automatically registered as Jews, their halakhic status remained in question. In 1985 the Chief Rabbinate ruled that, to marry, these Jews needed to undergo a lenient version of *giyyur le-humra* to remove doubts.[14] Some leaders of the Beta Israel community regarded this requirement as humiliating and racist because it was not imposed on other groups of immigrants. In protest, they organized an extended demonstration, which drew the issue of their status into the crosscurrents of broader political conflicts in Israel over the role of the Chief Rabbinate. An appeal to Israel's High Court eventually brought this episode, with its raw emotions, to some closure, removing the requirement of *giyyur le-humra* and granting the Ethiopian immigrants the same halakhic status as other Jewish immigrants: They would be regarded as Jews unless there were known issues of mixed lineage or divorce in their backgrounds.[15]

A different set of issues was posed by the Zera Beta Israel or Falashmura, descendants of the Beta Israel community who from the late nineteenth century onward converted to Christianity in waves, sometimes under intense pressure, but who subsequently lived in isolation from other Christian groups. In the wake of the mass immigration and absorption of the Beta Israel, members of the Falashmura sought to follow a similar path. The Ministry of Absorption set up several committees between 1991 and 2001 to study their history and make recommendations. The consensus was that to be recognized as Jews under the Law of Return members of this population would have to undergo a full but abbreviated conversion process. The continuing immigration of Falashmura, albeit in small numbers, remains controversial, given their very weak links to historic Judaism and the perception that they are primarily economic migrants seeking to improve their lives.[16]

Less well-known and fraught is the case of the Bnei Menashe of northeast India, whose ethnic origins are in the Shinlung tribes of the Indo-Burmese borderlands. Because there are so few members of this group and their presumptive Jewish roots are so elusive, they have remained mostly under the radar. Their path to *giyyur* appears to have begun in the 1890s when their homeland came under British colonial rule and Protestant missionaries began promoting literacy and Christianity. Missionaries who viewed the Shinlung through the lens of their own millenarian expectations may have suggested to them their origins in the Lost Tribes.[17] Some of the Shinlung whom the missionaries baptized subsequently became dissatisfied with Christianity because of its close association with British colonial rule. In 1951—only three years after Jewish resistance to British rule contributed to the departure of the British from Palestine and the establishment of a Jewish state—a Shinlung mystic reported dreaming that the Shinlung were descended from the Israelites. This belief spread quickly and was elaborated in a pamphlet literature that, among other claims, conflated the pre-Christian name of a Shinlung ancestral figure (Manasia) with the "lost" Israelite tribe Menashe.

In 1979, communal leaders of the Bnei Menashe established ties with the religious Zionist rabbi Eliyahu Avichail, a disciple of Zvi Yehudah Kook, who avidly sought out and proselytized among remote groups he believed had origins in the Lost Tribes. With the support of Avichail's organization Amishav, small numbers of Bene Menashe began arriving in Israel in 1989 on tourist visas. After studying for *giyyur* and undergoing conversion under the Chief Rabbinate, they qualified for citizenship under the Law of Return. In 2004 the well-funded group Shavei Israel took over, arranging for Orthodox conversions of Bnei Menashe in India. The Indian government objected, however, to what it regarded as proselytizing activity, which is prohibited by Indian law. Subsequently, small numbers of Bnei Menashe traveled to Nepal, where they underwent Orthodox conversion by Israeli rabbis sent for the purpose. They were then allowed to immigrate under the Law of Return to Israel, where most of the several hundred converts have settled in the West Bank.[18]

There are similarities in the trajectories of two other geographically remote judaizing groups whose members underwent *giyyur*—groups that, in contrast to those discussed earlier, made no claims to Jewish ancestry. In both cases, self-taught charismatic religious seekers, inspired by an unschooled reading of Scripture, persuaded villagers in their impoverished communities to adopt Jewish practices and abandon Catholicism. The contacts they established with Jews in the outside world eventually led to the rabbinically supervised conversion of their followers. The more recent of the two groups coalesced around a spiritually restless carpenter in the Peruvian Andes, Segundo Villanueva, whose unquiet mind accompanied him to the grave despite his conversion and immigration to Israel in 1989–1990. His followers settled in Israel in three small waves between 1990 and 2006.[19]

More fully documented is a case that unfolded against the backdrop of World War II. In the 1930s, a war-wounded folk healer named Donato Manduzio, from the poverty-stricken village of San Nicandro in southern Italy, obtained an Italian translation of the Bible from local Pentecostalists. Driven by a wish to understand suffering in the world, filled with unwavering self-confidence (reinforced by what he experienced as divine revelation), and convinced that Christians had erred in regarding Jesus as the messiah, he persuaded fellow villagers to convert to a belief and practice based on his reading of Scripture. His efforts to contact and gain support from Jews outside his narrow world—both Italian communal rabbis and Jewish officers fighting with the British—were met with caution, but Manduzio was nothing if not persistent. He importuned his Jewish contacts, who were at the time occupied with aiding Jewish refugees who had flooded southern Italy, to support the emigration of his followers to Palestine. Bitter internal feuding within his community complicated the task, but eventually circumcision was performed for those who sought it, and formal conversion followed. Serendipitously, Jewish efforts on behalf of refugees, along with the establishment of the Jewish state, created the networks and conditions that made possible the immigration of several dozen San Nicandresi converts to Israel in 1948 and 1949.[20]

"Emerging Jews" entered the contemporary Jewish world after modern transportation and communications made possible regular and ongoing contacts between remote groups and mainstream Jews. Zionist ideology, with its theme of the ingathering of the exiles, and the establishment of the State of Israel, with its mission of facilitating immigration, provided the external impetus for the religious and identitarian transformation of such groups. Consciously or unconsciously, the myth of the restoration of the Lost Tribes furnished practical efforts with mythic dimensions. The Jewish Agency and the nonprofit organization Shavei Israel were among the bodies that intervened actively to supply instruction and resources. In recent decades, internet websites and heritage tourism have also played a role in shaping the practice and self-understanding of these communities. In the media and popular consciousness the "judaization" of these communities has tended to be represented sentimentally, but scholarly studies based on fieldwork have provided some correction, throwing light on the sometimes painful and conflict-ridden processes of adaptation and religious conversion (in the broadest sense of the word) that Jews from these communities have undergone.

PART III

IN A NEW KEY

10 *Thinking About Jewish Conversion in the Twenty-First Century*

How scholars think about Jewish "conversion" has shifted in recent decades in ways that reflect broader trends in the methodologies and approaches of scholars in the humanities. This chapter discusses three major shifts and their impact on the study of conversion. Yet changes in the way recent scholars evaluate the various phenomena of Jewish conversion are not just methodological. Particularly where apostasy is concerned, there has been a marked alteration in scholarly sensibilities and attitudes. Let me share a few words on that subject before turning to new methodological approaches.

Until the 1980s, there was often a strong ideological thrust accompanied by stark value judgments in the scholarly representation of Jewish conversions "out," particularly to Christianity. Certainly, there were exceptions to the value-laden attitude that prevailed. Notable for its matter-of-factness, for example, was Jacob Katz's classic discussion of the halakhic status of apostates.[1] But as a rule, scholars viewed Jewish apostasy through the lens of their nationalist and religious loyalties.

In the last few decades scholars have increasingly dealt with conversion "out" as an integral aspect of ordinary Jewish (and human) experience. Scholars have shown that even in medieval and early modern Ashkenaz where religious boundaries were sharply drawn, voluntary apostasy was a fact of everyday life, even if the numbers were small.[2] As scholars explored the circumstances around voluntary conversion—among them poverty, personal entanglements, and criminal charges—they gave apostates a human face. Baptism, moreover, was not necessarily an irreversible step, as the many cases of baptized Jews who returned to the Jewish community attest.[3] Since the 1970s, studies of the medieval Geniza orbit, where Jews who chose to islamize often remained in contact with members of the Jewish community and sometimes returned to that community, also served to temper the image of the apostate as a cold-hearted opportunist.

Of particular importance in the modern period is the work of Todd Endelman, who has emphasized the novelty of the modern environment in which a Jew can leave Jewish life without converting to another religion and in which individual freedom is a primary value. Reflecting the less judgmental outlook of his generation, his starting point in discussing "radical assimilation" (whether involving conversion or not) is the universal human desire to secure happiness, the search for which, in modern societies, with their guarantee of religious freedom, is seen as an almost sacred right.[4]

In the current globalized, multicultural academic environment (which admittedly is now under considerable strain), the very concept of "apostasy," with its pejorative connotations, has lost some of its currency. An assumption prevails that human beings are free agents whose religious choices should be respected, rather than members of a religious collective to which they are responsible. Yet even though scholars may avoid the loaded term "apostasy," they continue to take an interest in the way people exit from religious communities and in how they enter new ones. Indeed, the editors of a recent collected volume (which includes studies of Jewish topics) have suggested a new field that they call "leaving religion," which would be devoted to theoretical and cross-cultural examination of the many ways in which people abandon religious traditions.[5]

Cross-Cultural and Comparative Approaches

Until the 1970s, work in the field of Jewish conversion was conducted almost entirely within the confines of Jewish institutions and was dominated by men with rabbinic training. A search on RAMBI (Index of Articles on Jewish Studies) confirms the impression that the most common area of research on conversion to Judaism up to that time was legal history—the study of the halakha of *giyyur*. Some studies had a historical focus; others analyzed contemporary issues and were published in journals with a denominational orientation.

As Jewish Studies scholars in the United States entered mainstream academia and as Israeli scholars followed the work of their American colleagues, the parameters of study began to shift. This is not to say that the number of intramural analyses of the practice and halakha of *giyyur* declined. On the contrary: Because the basic institutional procedures for conversion remained in place, with rabbis as the gatekeepers, and because issues of intermarriage and denominational difference lost none of their urgency, discussions of halakhic opinion continued to occupy a prominent place in the literature. But alongside these investigations appeared increasing numbers of studies that examined cases of conversion in their social, cultural, religious, and historical context, opening the way for comparison with non-Jewish patterns of conversion. The challenge in a multicultural academic environment has been finding a way to embrace insights drawn from other cultural settings without losing sight of the particularistic contours of Jewish experience.

This problem was not unique to Jewish Studies. By the early twenty-first century, general research on religious conversion was a rapidly growing field, and cross-cultural collections began to proliferate.[6] Yet it remained difficult to pin down a useful common conceptualization of religious conversion, and few ventured to undertake anything that might be called a genuinely comparative study.[7] At conferences and in collected volumes, scholars of various religious traditions, including Judaism, presented case studies raising questions about conversion that spanned eras, geographical space, and religious cultures. As Jewish Studies scholars were exposed to research that dealt with conversion in non-Jewish contexts, as well as to broader recent trends in the humanities, they found common analytic ground, and this inevitably informed their work. For example, like their colleagues in other fields, they discovered that premodern ethnoreligious boundaries were a good deal more fluid than had been assumed by an earlier generation of scholars. Although conversion could entail a dramatic, all-encompassing break with a prior religious community (as when a Christian cleric converted to Judaism and fled to a Jewish community in a Muslim land), it was often, as we have seen in these pages, a far more mundane experience—and this has been recognized as a general finding across cultures.

The collections that resulted from cross-cultural collaborations, despite their inevitably motley character and the flattening tendency of their introductions, served to broaden the contours of shared knowledge about the way people move from one religious culture to another. Yet breadth has its own limitations, as demonstrated by a volume with a particularly global reach, *The Anthropology of Religious Conversion* (2003). The contributions in this work include cases from across the globe. Among them, two case studies that involve conversions to Judaism—one dealing with the Falashmura of Ethiopia, the other with Gentiles undergoing *giyyur* to marry Jews in Copenhagen—illustrate the vastly different phenomena that comprise conversion within even a single religious tradition and underscore the hazards of comparison and generalization about conversion among different religious traditions.

Collaborative work has been most fruitful when the orbit of research has been more tightly circumscribed. Particularly productive have been studies that analyzed conversion among Jews, Christians, and Muslims in medieval and early modern Iberia.[8] An unusual contribution to this literature is James Amelang's genuinely comparative work analyzing two "parallel histories" in Spain—that of (a) forcibly baptized Jews and their descendants, and that of (b) forcibly baptized Muslims and their descendants. Until not so long ago, research on these two populations of forced converts developed along almost entirely independent lines. Yet as Amelang's work shows, they had many commonalities because of the similarities of the Spanish state's policies toward judeo-conversos and *moriscos* and of popular attitudes to the two populations.[9]

Undoubtedly, the mass forced conversions of two minority populations living in a single cultural space constitute a very unusual case that singularly lends itself to comparison. Yet even in the best of cases, scholars with a comparative agenda must try to balance the search for synthesis across cultures with the need to recognize cultural particularities that may be of the profoundest importance.

Identity Studies

In recent decades scholars have increasingly examined episodes of Jewish conversion through the lens of identity. To understand this transformation, it is worth recalling a time when Jewish identity was taken for granted as something intrinsic to "born Jews" or as something (an exceptional occurrence) that converts could acquire. This reflected a more general way of seeing groups as having inherent, unchanging, and clearly identifiable characteristics, which today is roundly rejected as "essentialist."

The dismantling of essentialist assumptions took place with startling rapidity in the late twentieth century because of developments in social psychology, anthropology, and political science. I would note two important milestones: Erik Erikson's examination of identity in the 1960s as a self-concept that was subject to instability and confusion, and Benedict Anderson's 1983 work *Imagined Communities*, which initiated a lively conversation about the way national groups create an idealized collective self-image. Identity was construed as a multidimensional construction, one that was in flux and always evolving in relation to perceptions of "the other." Identity studies had obvious applications for the study of Jewish conversion, and they have informed scholars' approaches when examining both Jewish attitudes to conversion and the way converts themselves have understood their passage from the Gentile to the Jewish world.

The identity issues underlying the rabbinic institution of a process for transforming Gentiles into Jews have been an especially strong area of scholarly interest. From ancient times, Jewish texts attest to the tension between a binary view of "us" and "them"—of Jew and Gentile as ontologically different beings—and the experienced reality of Gentiles who possessed qualities that Jews associated with themselves.[10] Shaye Cohen, in his seminal work *The Beginnings of Jewishness* (1999), undertook to study the historical processes that led to "the emergence of the possibility that a gentile could be enfranchised as a citizen in the household of Israel, either politically or religiously."[11] He and others have argued that Jewish exposure to Greek notions of citizenship and the adoption of Greek culture by non-Greeks opened up the possibility in the Jewish imagination for non-Jews to become Jews in a similar way.[12]

Yet Jewish concepts of genealogical identity and purity did not always allow for such a transformation. This issue drove an internal debate in Second Temple and early rabbinic circles to which scholars have also given close attention. The implications for conversion were critical. When Gentile impurity was seen to be of a moral or ritual character, it was mutable, and a Gentile could become a Jew through moral reform or a ritual process. When, however, it was seen to be genealogical and inherent, there was no mechanism by which this transformation could take place.[13] In the last few years scholars have continued to explore the paths opened by the initial discussion of these issues.[14]

For medievalists and early modernists, analysis of the evidence has increasingly challenged the assumption of stable and secure Jewish identities. Although the medieval religious, social, and psychic boundaries separating Jews from Christians were indeed profound—certainly when compared with other periods—the act of crossing those boundaries through conversion (mainly by Jewish apostates in this period) did not necessarily offer a secure alternative nor could it erase previous attachments. Research has revealed the instability of identity among ordinary Ashkenazi Jews who voluntarily accepted baptism to avoid special taxes, marry, escape family problems, or join the dominant religion. Although the act of conversion was presented by religious authorities as a total reorganization of the self, voluntary converts often found themselves denied full acceptance, while forced converts faced severe disorientation. Both in Christian Europe and in the Geniza world, apostates frequently returned to the Jewish community, with or without a ritual act to mark their return.[15]

The theme of unstable identities that runs through recent research on issues around conversion has special resonance for early modern Europe. There was a time when Jewish Studies scholars viewed the Reformation in northern Europe as an upheaval that had little to do with the Jews at all, except insofar as anti-Jewish rhetoric sharpened on both sides of the Protestant–Catholic divide. The boundaries for "Counter-Reformation" Europe were often (though not always) demarcated with similar clarity: Forcibly baptized Jews and their descendants were portrayed as victims of classic anti-Judaism and as ardent crypto-Jews, with the exception of the opportunists who joined the ranks of anti-Jewish polemicists.

Although boundary enforcement ("confessionalization") and inquisitorial efforts to remove judaizing heresy from Christian society were part of the early modern landscape, they were only partially effective. The very fact that they were felt to be necessary underscored the severity of the destabilization of religious identities—Jewish, Catholic, and Protestant alike. Especially in the last two decades, scholars have recognized and documented the role Jews played in the fluid religious crosscurrents of early modern Europe.[16] Paradoxically, in this environment of intense religious ferment, which witnessed a wide spectrum of Jewish religious behaviors, Jews were sometimes represented as essentially unchangeable—an idea that assumed an especially ideological cast in Iberia, where the impulse to "judaize" could be viewed as arising from Jewish "blood," rendering baptism seemingly ineffectual.[17] Such confidence in the fixity of Jewishness was, of course, an ideological fantasy that flew in the face of reality.

Although in recent years historians studying conversion have increasingly absorbed insights from identity theory, anthropologists have most consistently made that theory the framework for their studies. In the last chapter we discussed results of ethnographic fieldwork among the Beta Israel, Falashmura, Bnei Menashe, Portuguese urban Marranos, and immigrants from the Former Soviet Union.[18] All these studies involve populations of "emerging" Jews, and except for the Portuguese Marranos, the subjects of study were observed as they navigated their way amid the efforts of Jewish organizations and the Israeli state bureaucracy to reshape their religious, national, and cultural Gestalt. The overall approach to identity formation in these studies draws from approaches widely adopted in contemporary ethnographic literature. To convert, from such a perspective, is a process of many adjustments, some of which are unconscious and have little to do with the instruction converts receive about the tradition they are joining. It is, to quote one ethnographer, "to learn a new set of rules of behavior and vocabulary; to discover implicit structures of power and prestige, as well as explicit hierarchies; . . . and to position oneself and be positioned according to that world's available categories and relationships."[19] It also, of course, involves fashioning a coherent personal narrative with religious and mythic elements—a story, that is, about identity transformation.

Issues for Further Research

The aim of this book has been to acquaint readers with the many faces of "conversion" in Jewish life, past and present, drawing on scholarship in a variety of disciplines. Of course, there remain questions that cannot be answered because we lack adequate documentation. But there are also important questions that call for further study. Let me conclude this book with a discussion of a few directions for future research.

In popular consciousness, the premodern apostate has been envisioned as a Jew who turned his back entirely on the Jewish community, even engaging in anti-Jewish preaching and polemics. An older generation of historians lent credibility to that perception by largely ignoring ordinary cases of apostasy, regarding them as marginal to Jewish history. Changing sensibilities and interest in new evidentiary sources, however, have altered old assumptions about the supposed totality and finality of conversion "out." As discussed earlier, in recent decades scholars have contributed to a perception of less rigid Jewish–Gentile boundaries in both Christian and Muslim environments. A global overview of Jewish apostasy in its revised and more complex contours would thus seem a desideratum, perhaps in the form of a collaborative project bringing together scholars who study different populations of medieval and early modern Jews.

The asymmetric power relations between Jews and non-Jews in most of postbiblical history have meant that the typical features of Jewish apostasy, on the one hand, and of *giyyur*, on the other, are strikingly different. A primarily religious motivation behind conversion has been more apparent among *gerei tzedek* than among the far more numerous Jewish apostates. In the Christian world, the spiritual impetus for conversion was often related to familiarity with Scripture. Indeed, the role of the Old Testament/Hebrew Bible in the crystallization of thinking among Christian converts to Judaism runs like a thread through the history of *giyyur* from the medieval period to the present. A number of such cases have been discussed in this book. It was no accident that in the medieval European orbit converts to Judaism were usually clerics or educated men, whose reading of Scripture was key to their rejection of Christianity. In the early modern period, a new Protestant focus on the Old Testament and the religious uncertainties of Reformation Christianity led a few Christian religious seekers—among them Christian Hebraists—to gravitate to the seemingly stable world of Hebrew Scripture and rabbinic Judaism. In the nineteenth century, prophetic promises of the restoration of the Jews to Zion inspired Christian millenarians, among them the well-known convert Warder Cresson. Christian missionary activity far from the centers of Jewish life likely laid the foundations of "judaizing" movements among the Bnei Menashe in northeast India and the Beta Israel in Ethiopia. In the twentieth century, two charismatic Bible-reading spiritual leaders—one in rural Peru, the other in rural Italy—persuaded villagers in their poverty-stricken communities to abandon Catholicism and follow their scripturally informed understanding of Judaism; eventually they and their followers underwent formal *giyyur* and settled in Israel. These episodes suggest the rich material that might inform an analysis of the disparate ways in which the Hebrew Bible has been understood and mobilized by Christians who were moved to convert to Judaism.

In the modern period, no single development in the matter of *giyyur* has been more important than the establishment of the State of Israel. Scholars have discussed in some detail the issues that have arisen, some of which have aroused intense public scrutiny. However, much important research on this topic is in Hebrew and thus inaccessible to most American readers. It also tends to be oriented to policy, rather than to historical interpretation. There is unfortunately no single work that offers a judicious overview of a complex history that has touched on some of the most sensitive issues of contemporary Jewish life. Such a work would need to analyze the forces at work in the development of Israel's basic institutions, which have produced the confusing situation we discussed, in which one arm of the government (the civil administration) may recognize a person as Jewish while another (the Chief Rabbinate) regards them as a Gentile. A study of developments in Israel would also have to follow the course of efforts to gain civil recognition in Israel for conversions performed by non-Orthodox Jewish rabbis and religious courts, whether abroad or in Israel. It would need to trace various efforts, beginning in the 1960s and continuing today, to make possible Orthodox conversions in Israel outside the purview of the Chief Rabbinate (albeit without the latter's recognition). It would also need to chart the issues arising from the mass immigration to Israel under the Law of Return of persons from the Former Soviet Union who are fully integrated into Jewish Israeli society but are Gentiles according to Jewish law. It would ideally deal with the increasing pressure the Chief Rabbinate has placed on Orthodox rabbis abroad to adhere to their standards of *giyyur*. Most importantly, such a work would contextualize these developments within the changing ideological, demographic, and political contours of Israeli society.

Another area that calls for investigation is the striking gender imbalance in twentieth- and twenty-first-century conversions to Judaism, with women converts far outnumbering men both in the United States and Israel (and presumably elsewhere as well). Because most conversions occur in the context of marriage to a Jew, it seems possible that gender differences in patterns of family formation may lead women to favor (or be amenable to) becoming Jewishly involved, whereas men may be more apt to resist doing so. Men whose self-image is closely tied up with competency in the workplace may find intimidating the expectation of facility with traditional Hebrew texts and ritual practices that is associated with male competence in Jewish life, whether in the synagogue, at the seder table, or in the study hall. Women, in contrast, with their orientation to the realm of the household where they continue to hold sway, may be especially attracted to Jewish ritual practices that infuse everyday life with emotional and spiritual resonance.[20] But this is only a suggestion, not the conclusive result of a study, and the question remains open.

The social and religious "afterlife" of conversions is an area that has been neglected, in my view. It may have been natural for scholars to focus on the better-documented issues around the initial acceptance of converts and to overlook what is ultimately the most creative work of conversion, which is done by converts themselves in the years and decades after their *giyyur*. How have they integrated into the Jewish communities they joined? What challenges have they faced, as converts, in a Jewish culture that is still oriented toward an ancestral definition of Jewishness? How have they negotiated holidays and life-cycle events with members of their birth families? What has been the experience of children who were converted at an impressionable age—typically, children of female converts from previous marriages or non-Jewish children adopted by Jews? What have those converted in childhood done when, at bat mitzvah or bar mitzvah age, they were given the option of confirming or rejecting their conversions? It is true that these issues have little bearing on the burning political and ideological issues of contemporary Jewish life. Yet they are very much part of the human landscape of the contemporary Jewish world in which conversion is an increasingly quotidian occurrence.

Notes

INTRODUCTION

1. Karl Morrison, *Understanding Conversion* (University of Virginia Press, 1992), xv.

2. William James, *Varieties of Religious Experience* (Longmans, Green, and Co., 1902), 189. And see Arthur Darby Nock, *Conversion: The Old and the New in Religion from Alexander the Great to Augustine of Hippo* (Oxford University Press, 1933).

3. Heinrich Graetz, *Geschichte der Juden von den ältesten Zeiten bis auf die Gegenwart*, 11 vols. (O. Leiner, 1866–1878).

4. See, for example, the essays in Lewis Rambo and Charles Farhadian, *The Oxford Handbook of Religious Conversion* (Oxford University Press, 2014). For an example in the realm of Jewish Studies, see Theodor Dunkelgrün and Paweł Maciejko, eds., *Bastards and Believers: Jewish Converts and Conversion from the Bible to the Present* (University of Pennsylvania, 2020).

5. Lewis Rambo, *Understanding Religious Conversion* (Yale University Press, 1993), xiv. Emphasis mine.

6. Historically, because of censorship of Hebrew books, Hebrew printers replaced the term *meshumad* with the term *mumar* (from the same root as *hamarah*). See Solomon Zeitlin, "*Mumar* and *Meshumad*," *Jewish Quarterly Review* 54, no. 1 (1963): 84.

7. See Todd Endelman, "Welcoming Ex-Jews into the Jewish Historiographical Fold," in idem, *Broadening Jewish History: Towards a Social History of Ordinary Jews* (Oxford University Press, 2011), 82–92.

8. On this rabbinic principle see Jacob Katz, "Even Though a Sinner, He Is Still of Israel," *Tarbiz* 27 (1958): 203–227 [in Hebrew].

9. Such cases are admittedly rare. For a rabbinic analysis, see Aharon Lichtenstein, "Brother Daniel and the Jewish Fraternity," *Judaism* 12, no. 3 (1963): 263–268. For an analysis of the secular legal situation, see Bernard S. Jackson, "Brother Daniel: The Construction of Jewish Identity in the Israel Supreme Court," *Revue internationale de semiotique juridique* 6, no. 2 (1993): 115–146.

10. The source for this is the Babylonian Talmud, Megillah 17b.

CHAPTER 1 — BIBLICAL PERIOD

1. I use here the term "a person of non-Israelite origin" rather than "Gentile" because before the early rabbinic period the term *goy* was used exclusively to mean

"nation" (e.g., *goy kadosh*). There was no Hebrew term for a Gentile person. For a detailed discussion of this, see Adi Ophir and Ishay Rosen-Zvi, *Goy: Israel's Multiple Others and the Birth of the Gentile* (Oxford University Press 2020).

2. For discussion of the term *ger* I relied on Sara Japhet, "The Term *Ger* and the Concept of Conversion in the Hebrew Bible," in *Bastards and Believers: Jewish Converts and Conversion from the Bible to the Present*, ed. Theodor Dunkelgrün and Pawel Maciejko (University of Pennsylvania Press, 2020), 26–41; Ophir and Rosen-Zvi, *Goy*, 23–56; and Nadav Na'aman, "Sojourners and Levites in the Kingdom of Judah in the Seventh Century BCE," *Zeitschrift für altorientalische und biblische Rechtsgeschichte* 14 (2008): 237–259.

3. For a discussion of why such a circumcision in this instance cannot be understood as a conversion ritual, see Matthew Thiessen, *Contesting Conversion: Genealogy, Circumcision, and Identity in Ancient Judaism and Christianity* (Oxford University Press, 2011), 60–63.

4. Ruth Rabbah 2:22.

5. On the various prohibited marriages in the Pentateuch, see Shaye Cohen, *The Beginnings of Jewishness: Boundaries, Varieties, Uncertainties* (University of California Press, 1999), 242–262. In the biblical narrative, violations of these restrictions could bring reproach. Thus, for example, King Solomon was rebuked for marrying Moabite, Ammonite, Edomite, Sidonian, and Hittite wives, for the explicit reason that his doing so could lead to idolatry among his people (I Kings 11:2).

6. See Joel Kaminsky, "A Light to the Nations: Was There Mission and /or Conversion in the Hebrew Bible?" *Jewish Studies Quarterly* 16, no. 1 (2009): 9.

7. For a summary of the various problems in the text, see Lester Grabbe, *A History of the Jews and Judaism in the Second Temple Period*, vol. 1 (T. & T. Clark, 2004), 70–85.

8. The intermarriage of the descendants of the high priest Joshua is mentioned in Ezra 10:18. For a discussion of the composition of the local population—referred to as the *"amei ha-aretz"*—see Sara Japhet, "People and Land in the Restoration Period," in idem, *From the Rivers of Babylon to the Highlands of Judah* (Penn State University Press, 2021), 96–116, esp. 111–113.

9. As Morton Smith noted, "That the aliens involved in the mixed marriages might become proselytes—that is, might accept the obligations of the law and also receive its benefits, including purification—was something Ezra never considered." Morton Smith, *Palestinian Parties and Politics That Shaped the Old Testament* (SCM Press, 1987), 137.

10. See Saul Olyan, "Purity Ideology in Ezra-Nehemiah as a Tool to Reconstitute the Community," *Journal for the Study of Judaism* 35, no. 1 (2004): 2–3.

11. On the exclusivist policy of Ezra-Nehemiah see, inter alia, Ophir and Rosen-Zvi, *Goy*, 57–74; Olyan, "Purity Ideology," 1–16; and Christine Hayes, *Gentile Impurities and Jewish Identities: Intermarriage and Conversion from the Bible to the Talmud* (Oxford University Press, 2002), 26–33.

CHAPTER 2 — SECOND TEMPLE

1. See Christine Hayes, *Gentile Impurities and Jewish Identities: Intermarriage and Conversion from the Bible to the Talmud* (Oxford University Press, 2002), 73–81; Ophir and Rosen-Zvi, *Goy*, 86–109.

2. On the vexing problem of what this term meant see, inter alia, Daniel Schwartz, *Judeans and Jews: Four Faces of Dichotomy in Ancient Jewish History* (University of Toronto Press, 2014), 3–20; Steve Mason, "Jews, Judaeans, Judaizing, Judaism: Problems of Categorization in Ancient History," *Journal for the Study of Judaism* 38, nos. 4–5 (2007): 457–512.

3. This differentiated it from hellenization, which entailed certain pressures but not coercion. The infamous persecutions of Antiochus IV were a fleeting episode in the long historical encounter of Jews with Hellenistic culture. Traditional lore notwithstanding, the Maccabees were not cultural purists and did not go to war against Greek culture.

4. Shaye Cohen, *The Beginnings of Jewishness: Boundaries, Varieties, Uncertainties* (University of California Press, 1999), 110–129.

5. Shaye Cohen has vividly illustrated the difficulty of assigning Herod a coherent identity. See Cohen, *Beginnings of Jewishness*, 13–24.

6. Some Idumeans did, however, refuse to accept the imposition of Torah law, secretly practicing their ancestral cult or fleeing to Egypt where they could do so openly. See Seth Schwartz, *Imperialism and Jewish Society, 200 B.C.E. to 640 C.E.* (Princeton University Press, 2004), 37–38, 51–52.

7. Josephus, *Antiquities of the Jews*, 14:15.

8. On the integration as Jews of Idumeans and others see Cohen, *Beginnings of Jewishness*, 81–82,109–119, 125–129; Schwartz, *Imperialism*, 22–28, 32–42; Benedikt Eckhardt, "'An Idumean, That Is, a Half-Jew': Hasmoneans and Herodians Between Ancestry and Merit," in *Jewish Identity and Politics Between the Maccabees and Bar Kokhba*, ed. B. Eckhardt (Brill, 2012), 91–115.

9. See Cohen, *Beginnings of Jewishness*, 156–162.

10. Terence Donaldson, "Jerusalem Ossuary Inscriptions and the Status of Jewish Proselytes," in *Text and Artifact in the Religions of Mediterranean Antiquity: Essays in Honour of Peter Richardson*, ed. Peter Richardson (Wilfrid Laurier University Press, 2000), 372–388.

CHAPTER 3 — RABBINIC

1. The Jerusalem Talmud, or "Yerushalmi," has a secondary status.

2. For a dire assessment of post-destruction realities under Roman rule, see Seth Schwartz, *Imperialism and Jewish Society* (Princeton University Press, 2004),103–165.

For a critique of this view, see Michael Satlow's review in *Jewish Quarterly Review* 95, no. 1 (2005): 160–161.

3. On known incidents of conversion, see Bernard Jacob Bamberger, *Proselytism in the Talmudic Period* (Ktav, 1939), 221–266; Isaiah Gafni, *The Jews of Babylonia in the Talmudic Era* [Hebrew] (Mercaz Shazar 1990), 137–148; cf. Shaye Cohen, *The Beginnings of Jewishness* (University of California Press, 1999), 330.

4. See, inter alia, Catherine Hezser, *The Social Structure of the Rabbinic Movement in Roman Palestine* (Mohr Siebeck, 1997).

5. Mishnah Yevamot 2:8.

6. This is noted by Avi Sagi and Zvi Zohar, *Transforming Identity: The Ritual Transition from Gentile to Jew, Structure and Meaning* (Continuum, 2007), 9. The phrase first appears in the talmudic tractate Gerim.

7. Babylonian Talmud (BT) Yevamot 24b and Palestinian Talmud Kiddushin 4.1. See Sagi and Zohar, *Transforming Identity*, 10–11.

8. Tosefta Demai 2:5: "A convert who takes upon himself all the obligations of the Torah, and is suspected about one of them, or even the entire Torah, behold, he is considered a Jewish apostate."

9. BT Yevamot 24b.

10. BT Ketubot 11a. On the conversion of minors see Joshua Kulp, "The Participation of a Court in the Jewish Conversion Process," *Jewish Quarterly Review* 94 (2004): 459–469.

11. BT Yevamot 47a-b. Another description in Gerim 1:1 is based on Yevamot, with significant differences. Shaye Cohen argues that the Yevamot text is a Baraita of the second or early third century C.E. For a comparison of the two texts see Cohen, *Beginnings*, 198–217; Sagi and Zohar, *Transforming Identity*, 141–152. For a discussion of this entire passage see Moshe Lavee, "The 'Tractate' of Conversion—BT Yeb. 46–48 and the Evolution of Conversion Procedure," *European Journal of Jewish Studies* 4, no. 2 (2010): 169–213.

12. In the case of a male convert who had already been circumcised, Beit Shammai was reported to have required *hatafat dam* (the drawing of a drop of blood from the site of circumcision), whereas Beit Hillel did not (BT Shabbat 135a). The current practice of requiring *hatafat dam* became definitive only in the sixteenth century, with the diffusion of the code known as the *Shulkhan Arukh* (Yoreh Deah 263:4).

13. Shaye Cohen suggests that the very establishment of immersion as part of the conversion process may have had something to do with the sensed need for a ritual for women. Cohen, *Beginnings*, 223.

14. BT Yevamot 46b. On this passage, see Lavee, "'Tractate' of Conversion," 185.

15. See Shaye Cohen, *Why Aren't Jewish Women Circumcised? Gender and Covenant in Judaism* (University of California Press, 2005); Sagi and Zohar, *Transforming Identity*, 116–131.

16. BT Yevamot 47b.

17. BT Sanhedrin 58b.

18. For example, Mishnah Bikkurim 1:4 refers to a convert who has an Israelite mother. See the detailed discussion in Cohen, *Beginnings*, 308–324.

19. On the prior absence of such a principle see Cohen, *Beginnings*, 268–273.

20. Sagi and Zohar, *Transforming Identity*, 145.

21. BT Shabbat 31a.

22. My emphasis. The Mishnaic scholar Yossi ben Rabbi Yehuda held that this instruction was to include even the smallest details of rabbinic law. On this maximalist position see Cohen, *Beginnings*, 229; Sagi and Zohar, *Transforming Identity*, 108–114.

23. Kulp, "Participation of a Court," 438.

24. BT Yevamot 47a.

25. The discrepancy between the requirement of "two rabbis" and the requirement of a court of three was resolved by R. Yohanan; see BT Yevamot 47b. On the introduction of the requirement of a court see Kulp, "Participation of a Court," 449–457; Lavee, "'Tractate' of Conversion," 186–188.

26. BT Yevamot 48b.

27. BT Bekhorot 47a.

28. An exception was made if she was converted before the age of three years and one day (BT Yevamot 60b; BT Kiddushin 78a).

29. For the biblical source, see Lev. 21:7.

30. See Mishnah Kiddushin 4:6–7. One opinion in this passage held that for even up to ten generations the offspring of a female convert could not marry a priest. Such an extreme ruling, if enforced, would have required genealogical recordkeeping and sustaining a Jewish subgroup that included persons of remote Gentile ancestry.

31. Mishnah Bikkurim 1:4–5 and cf. Mishnah Ma'aser Sheni 5:14.

32. BT Makkot 19a. See Cohen, *Beginnings*, 330 n46.

33. Yerushalmi Bikkurim 1:4. For an analysis of the passage see Cohen, *Beginnings*, 328–329.

34. Genesis Rabbah 39:15. The trope of Abraham's spiritual fatherhood of the convert was given new expression in the medieval period when it became the custom to name the convert "so-and-so son/daughter of our father Abraham."

35. The origin of this expression is Ruth 2:12. For early rabbinic expressions see Avot de Rabbi Nathan, chap. 12; Shabbat 31a; Sanhedrin 96b; Sifra Kedoshim, chap. 8.

36. Avot de Rabbi Nathan, chap. 12.

37. BT Pesahim 87b.

38. BT Shabbat 31a. And see the story of Timna who was disastrously turned away in BT Sanhedrin 99b.

39. BT Yevamoth 47b; Ruth Rabbah 2:22.

40. Midrash Tanhuma, Parshat Lech Lecha 6 (Buber edition).

41. BT Shevuot 39a.

42. BT Gittin 57b. Similar traditions held that the emperor Nero and Nebuchadnezzar's guard became proselytes (Bamidbar Rabbah 19:32; BT Sanhedrin 96b); the Bible translator and convert Onkelos was said to be a nephew of Titus, the Roman commander who destroyed the Temple (BT Gittin 46b-47a).

43. BT Yevamot 47b. R. Helbo derived the image of the scab (*sappaḥat*, with its root SPH) from the verse "And the convert [*ger*] shall join himself with them, and they shall cleave [*veniSPeHu*] to the house of Jacob" [Isaiah 14:1]. On the positive spin placed on this dictum by several tosafists, see Jacob Katz, *Exclusiveness and Tolerance: Studies in Jewish-Gentile Relations in Medieval and Modern Times* (Behrman House, 1961), 80–81.

44. BT Yevamot 109b. See also BT Niddah 13b, where R. Helbo's statement is again cited.

45. Rashi on Ex. 32:7; Shemot Rabbah 42:6.

46. For further examples see Paweł Maciejko, *The Mixed Multitude: Jacob Frank and the Frankist Movement, 1755–1816* (University of Pennsylvania Press, 2011), 2–6.

47. Mekhilta de R. Ishmael, Tractate Nezikin 18. In another source the injunction is made to cover even the less aggressive: "Yesterday you were an idolator, and today you have entered under the wings of the Divine Presence" (Sifra Kedoshim 8:2).

CHAPTER 4 — MEDIEVAL

1. The Karaites adhered to a movement that rejected postbiblical Judaism as it was developed by the rabbis and broke with rabbinic Judaism in the ninth century.

2. Tosefta Horayot 1:5 defines a *mumar* as someone "who eats carrion and non-kosher meat, *sheketzim* and *remasim* (detestable things), or pork, or who drinks forbidden wine or desecrates the Sabbath."

3. See, for example, BT Sanhedrin 27a and BT Avodah Zarah 26b.

4. For this view see Jacob Katz, *Exclusiveness and Tolerance* (Behrman House, 1961), 68–72; Gerald Blidstein, "Who Is Not a Jew? The Medieval Discussion," *Israel Law Review* 11, no. 3 (1976): 369–390.

5. On the topic of Ashkenazi rabbinic rulings about apostates (and returning apostates in particular), see Ephraim Kanarfogel, *Brothers from Afar: Rabbinic Approaches to Apostasy and Reversion in Medieval Europe* (Wayne State University Press, 2020).

6. Joshua Olsson, "Coup d'état, Coronation and Conversion: Some Reflections on the Adoption of Judaism by the Khazar Khaganate," *Journal of the Royal Asiatic Society* 23, no. 4 (2013): 498.

7. For a discussion of these practices see Peter Golden, "The Conversion of the Khazars to Judaism," in *The World of the Khazars: New Perspectives: Selected Papers from the Jerusalem 1999 International Khazar Colloquium*, vol. 17, ed. Peter Golden, Haggai Ben-Shammai, and András Róna-Tas (Brill, 2007), 130–135.

8. See Golden, "Conversion of the Khazars," 123–138.

9. Omeljan Pritsak, "The Khazar Kingdom's Conversion to Judaism," *Harvard Ukrainian Studies* 2, no. 3 (1978): 281.

10. Olsson, "Coup d'état," 508–517.

11. For a detailed discussion of the halakha governing the status that slaves assumed at the time of purchase and at the time of manumission, see Menachem Finkelstein, *Conversion: Halakhah and practice* (Bar-Ilan University Press, 2006), 108—158.

12. *Hilkhot Issurei Bi'ah*, 12: 11.

13. For a discussion of Jewish slave ownership under Islam in a later period see Yaron Ben-Naeh, "Blond, Tall, with Honey-Colored Eyes: Jewish Ownership of Slaves in the Ottoman Empire," *Jewish History* 20 (2006): 315–332.

14. On the ethnic origins of Egyptian slaves in this period, derived mainly from bills of sale, see Craig Perry, "The Daily Life of Slaves and the Global Reach of Slavery" (PhD diss., Emory University, 2014), 29–47, esp. 39. More than half the slaves identified in bills of sale were "Black" or "Nubian." For a list of 118 slaves mentioned in the Geniza, with a summary of data about them, see Perry, "Daily Life of Slaves," 225–230.

15. On the Islamic prohibition of religious minorities owning Muslim slaves, see Joseph Schacht, *An Introduction to Islamic Law* (Clarendon Press, 1964), 132.

16. Moshe Yagur, "Religious Identity and Communal Boundaries in Geniza Society (10th–13th Centuries): Proselytes, Slaves, Apostates" [in Hebrew] (PhD diss., Hebrew University 2017), 74.

17. Perry, "Daily Life of Slaves," 69.

18. Pierre Bourdieu, *Outline of a Theory of Practice* (Cambridge University Press, 1977), 33–38; cf. Perry, "Daily Life of Slaves," 68.

19. There was, however, a prohibition of selling a circumcised slave to a non-Jew. Yagur, "Religious Identity," 74.

20. For examples of the ties of affection between Jewish mistresses and their female slaves, see Shelomo Dov Goitein, *A Mediterranean Society: The Jewish Communities of*

the Arab World as Portrayed in the Documents of the Cairo Geniza, 5 vols. (University of California Press, 1999) 1:144–147; Perry, "Daily Life of Slaves," 66–70, 188–195.

21. See Craig Perry, "Conversion as an Aspect of Master–Slave Relationships in the Medieval Egyptian Jewish Community," in *Contesting Inter-Religious Conversion in the Medieval World*, ed. Yaniv Fox and Yosi Yisraeli (Routledge, 2017), 135–159.

22. Perry, "Daily Life of Slaves," 160.

23. On this practice see Perry, "Daily Life of Slaves," 107–153; Yagur, "Religious Identity," 101–115; Goitein, *Mediterranean Society* 1:134–135.

24. Maimonides, *Teshuvat Ha-Rambam*, ed. Joshua Blau (Mekitse Nirdamim, 1960), 3 vols., 2: no. 211.

25. Yagur, "Religious Identity," 42. Yagur has identified eleven complete *gittei shikhrur* in the Geniza.

26. On the integration of freed slaves and attitudes to them see Yagur, "Religious Identity," 88–100.

27. Yagur, "Religious Identity," 16, 19. Only seventy-some Geniza documents mention *gerim* at all. On converts mentioned in the Geniza, see Goitein, *Mediterranean Society*, 2:303–311; Moshe Yagur, "The Donor and the Gravedigger: Converts to Judaism in the Cairo Geniza Documents," in *Contesting Inter-Religious Conversion*, 115–126.

28. Yagur, "Religious Identity," 16–22.

29. On these converts and others mentioned in the Geniza, see Goitein, *Mediterranean Society*, 2:304–310; Yagur, "Donor and the Gravedigger," 122–142.

30. For examples of some relatively affluent proselytes, see Goitein, *Mediterranean Society*, 2:306–307.

31. On Abu al-Khayr, see Goitein, *Mediterranean Society*, 2:305–306.

32. "Our fathers have inherited nought but lies, worthless things in which there is no profit" (Jeremiah 16:19).

33. The discussion of this case is based on Moshe Yagur, "Captives, Converts, and Concubines: Gendered Aspects of Conversion to Judaism in the Medieval Near East," in *Language, Gender and Law in the Judaeo-Islamic Milieu*, ed. Zvi Stampfer and Amir Ashur (Brill, 2020), 88–109.

34. Yagur, "Captives," 91–92.

35. See Yosef Hayim Yerushalmi, "The Inquisition and the Jews of France in the Time of Bernard Gui," *Harvard Theological Review* 63, no. 3 (1970): 363–367.

36. For the early rabbinic sources see Mishnah Bikkurim 1:4; Yerushalmi Bikkurim 1:4, 64a. For the discussion of the Tosafists, see Ben Zion Wacholder, "Cases of Proselytizing in the Tosafist Responsa," *Jewish Quarterly Review* 51, no. 4 (1961): 301–302.

37. Maimonides, *Teshuvot ha-Rambam*, 2: no. 293.

38. Moshe Halbertal, *Maimonides: Life and Thought* (Princeton University Press, 2013), 82.

39. For a discussion of the discrepancy between the letter to Ovadiah and the exposition in the *Mishneh Torah*, see Menachem Lorberbaum, "Maimonides' Letter to Ovadyah: An Analysis," *S'vara* 3, no. 1 (1993): 61–62.

40. *Mishneh Torah, Hilkhot Issurei Biah* 13–14.

41. On the rare exceptions, see Sagi and Zohar, *Transforming Identity*, 27–29.

42. *Book of Kuzari* 1.27, Hartwig Hirschfeld translation.

43. *Book of Kuzari* 1.115.

44. Sarah Stroumsa, "On Jewish Intellectuals Who Converted in the Early Middle Ages," in *The Jews of Medieval Islam: Community, Society, and Identity*, ed. Daniel Frank (Brill, 1995), 185.

45. On the practical benefits of apostasy see Uriel Simonsohn, "Conversion, Exemption, and Manipulation: Social Benefits and Conversion to Islam in Late Antiquity and the Middle Ages," *Medieval Worlds* 6 (2017): 196–216.

46. For a discussion of geonic views in the realm of inheritance, see Oded Irshai, "The Apostate as an Inheritor in Geonic Responsa—Basics of Decision Making and Parallels in Gentile Law" [in Hebrew], *Shenaton ha-Mishpat ha-Ivri*, XI–XII (1984–1986): 435–461. For four examples of geonic responsa see Oded Zinger, "Apostasy in Jewish Responsa, by the Geonim of Babylonia and Abraham Maimonides," in *Conversion to Islam in the Premodern Age: A Sourcebook*, ed. Nimrod Hurvitz et al. (University of California Press, 2021), 220–226.

47. For examples, see Uriel Simonsohn, "The Legal and Social Bonds of Jewish Apostates and Their Spouses According to Gaonic Responsa," *Jewish Quarterly Review* 105, no. 4 (2015): 417–439, and Moshe Yagur, "Religiously Mixed Families in the Mediterranean Society of the Cairo Geniza," *Mediterranean Historical Review* 35, no. 1 (2020), 27–42.

48. See Moshe Yagur, "Excommunication and Apostasy: Re-Drawing Jewish Communal Boundaries in Fāṭimid and Ayyūbid Egypt," *Al-Masāq* 35, no. 1 (2023): 95–109.

49. Yagur, "Religiously Mixed Families," 29.

50. For an effort to address some of the issues surrounding such cases see Stroumsa, "Jewish Intellectuals," 179–197.

51. Yehoshua Frenkel, "The Conversion of ʿAbd al-Sayyid, a Damascene Jew," in *Conversion to Islam in the Premodern Age*, 272–274.

52. See Mark Cohen and Sasson Somekh, "In the Court of Ya'qūb Ibn Killis: A Fragment from the Cairo Genizah," *Jewish Quarterly Review* 80, nos. 3–4 (1990): 283–314, esp. 285–286. An additional source that depicts Ibn Killis in a polemical stance is Christian, but it depicts him as defending Judaism. According to this source, Ibn Killis interrupted a disputation between a Coptic Christian and a Jew when it became

evident that the Jewish disputant was losing; he took over the Jewish side of the debate, but—and this is the point of the story for the Christian audience—he himself was defeated by the Coptic patriarch.

53. There is a considerable scholarly literature on these figures, who include the possibly mythical Ka'b al-Ahbar (seventh century), as well as Said b. Hasan al-Iskandari (thirteenth and fourteenth centuries), and Abd al-Haqq al-Islami (late fourteenth century).

54. See Adnan Husain, "Conversion to History: Negating Exile and Messianism in al-Samaw'al al-Maghribi's Polemic Against Judaism," *Medieval Encounters* 8, no. 1 (2002): 3–34.

55. See Gregor Schwarb, "A Polemical Treatise by a Twelfth-Century Jewish Convert to Islam," in *Conversion to Islam in the Premodern Age,* 199–203.

56. See Yagur, "Religiously Mixed Families," 35. On Islamic theory and practice regarding apostates from Islam, see Antoine Fattal, *Le statut légal des non-musulmans en pays d'Islam* (Librairie Orientale, 1958), 163–168.

57. Rav Hayya Gaon ruled that "a person who apostatized while a mature adult, and later repented honestly, publicly and not secretly, is as legitimate [a Jew] as all others." Yagur, "Religiously Mixed Families," 30. On returnees to Judaism, see Uriel Simonsohn, "'Halting Between Two Opinions': Conversion and Apostasy in Early Islam," *Medieval Encounters* 19 (2013): 342–370.

58. See Yohanan Friedmann, *Tolerance and Coercion in Islam: Interfaith Relations in the Muslim Tradition* (Cambridge University Press, 2003), 144.

59. We will not deal with a brief episode that took place under the erratic Fatimid caliph Al-Hakim, 996–1013. On forced conversions in twelfth-century Yemen, see Yosef Tobi, "Conversion to Islam Among Yemenite Jews Under Zaydi Rule," in *The Legacy of Islamic Antisemitism: From Sacred Texts to Solemn History,* ed. Andrew Bostom (Prometheus Books, 2008), 577–578.

60. On this episode see H. Z. Hirschberg, *A History of the Jews in North Africa,* vol. 1 (Brill, 1974), 123–139.

61. On *taqiyya* see Devin Stewart, "Dissimulation in Sunni Islam and Morisco Taqiyya," *Al-qantara* 34, no. 2 (2013): 439–490.

62. The *shahada* in English translation is "There is no god but God [Allah], and Muhammad is the Messenger of God."

63. Hirschberg, *History of the Jews* 1:127–128.

64. See the English translation in Abraham S. Halkin and David Hartman, *Epistles of Maimonides: Crisis and Leadership* (Jewish Publication Society, 1993), 15–34.

65. Halkin and Hartman, *Epistles,* 16.

66. Halkin and Hartman, *Epistles,* 30.

67. For a discussion of the apparent lack of risk for converts in some contexts see Wacholder, "Cases of Proselytizing," 297, 308–310.

68. See Paola Tartakoff, *Conversion, Circumcision, and Ritual Murder in Medieval Europe* (University of Pennsylvania Press, 2020), 87–88.

69. Solomon Grayzel, *The Church and the Jews in the XIIIth Century*, rev. ed. (Hermon Press, 1966), 23 n5. See the case of Abraham ben Abraham of Augsburg, burned at the stake in 1264, in Paola Tartakoff, "Martyrdom, Conversion, and Shared Cultural Repertoires in Late Medieval Europe," *Jewish Quarterly Review* 109, no. 4 (2019): 500–503.

70. Such conversions were apparently rare enough that they did not prompt legislation, but a German regulation of 1325 stipulated, "No Jew shall convert a Christian to his faith; if he does, it costs his life." Guido Kisch, *The Jews in Medieval Germany: A Study of their Legal and Social Status* (University of Chicago, 1949), 200.

71. Grayzel, *Church and the Jews*, 22, n1. A thirteenth-century chronicle gives an account of a Jew executed for accepting a convert from Christianity; see Tartakoff, *Conversion, Circumcision*, 92.

72. On such fantasizing, which was sometimes linked to charges of ritual murder or host desecration, see Tartakoff, *Conversion, Circumcision*, 1–6, 18–69.

73. Tartakoff, *Conversion, Circumcision*, 70–71. This figure does not include the conversions of slaves.

74. Bernhard Blumenkranz, "Anti-Jewish Polemics and Legislation in the Middle Ages: Literary Fiction or Reality?" *Journal of Jewish Studies* 25 (1964): 125.

75. It is thus also no accident that converts of this type were almost invariably male. An exception may be the young noblewoman from northern Europe who, after her conversion around the time of the First Crusade, fled to Narbonne, where she married a local Jew. See Norman Golb, "Jewish Proselytism—A Phenomenon in the Religious History of Early Medieval Europe," *Tenth Annual Rabbi Louis Feinberg Memorial Lecture* (Hebrew Union College, 1987), 12–15.

76. For a discussion of this, see Avraham Reiner, "L'attitude envers les proselytes en Allemagne et en France du XIe au XIIIe siècle," *Revue des études juives* 167, nos. 1–2 (2008): 99–119, in which the author argues that there was a shift toward greater acceptance of proselytes in the late twelfth century. On the view that the *ger's* status was in some ineffable way distinct from that of other Jews see Ephraim Kanarfogel, "Approaches to Conversion in Medieval European Rabbinic Literature: From Ashkenaz to Sefarad," in *Conversion, Intermarriage, and Jewish Identity*, ed. Adam Mintz and Marc Stern (Ktav, 2015), 218–219.

77. See Kanarfogel, "Approaches to Conversion," 236–237.

78. See Kanarfogel, "Approaches to Conversion," 219–220.

79. For a survey of reports of *gerim* who were put to death by Christians see Tartakoff, *Conversion, Circumcision*, 84–86.

80. Adolf Neubauer, "Le Memorbuch de Mayence, Essai sur la Littérature des Complaintes," *Revue des études juives* 4 (1882): 13.

81. See Jochanan Wijnhoven, "The Zohar and the Proselyte," in *Readings on Conversion to Judaism*, ed. Lawrence Epstein (Jason Aronson, 1995), 47–65.

82. For cases mentioned in inquisitorial records, see Paola Tartakoff, *Between Christian and Jew: Conversion and Inquisition in the Crown of Aragon, 1250–1391* (University of Pennsylvania Press, 2012), 25.

83. See Frank Riess, "From Aachen to Al-Andalus: The Journey of Deacon Bodo (823–76)," *Early Medieval Europe* 13, no. 2 (2005): 131–157; Golb, "Jewish Proselytism," 2–4.

84. Anna Sapir Abulafia, "An Eleventh-Century Exchange of Letters Between a Christian and a Jew," *Journal of Medieval History* 7, no. 2 (1981): 153–174; and see Golb, "Jewish Proselytism," 4–8.

85. Shelomo Dov Goitein, "Obadya, a Norman Proselyte," *Journal of Jewish Studies* 4 (1953): 75.

86. On Ovadiah's account, see Joshua Prawer, "The Autobiography of Obadyah the Norman, a Convert to Judaism at the Time of the First Crusade," in *Studies in Medieval Jewish History and Literature*, vol. I, ed. Isadore Twersky (Harvard University Press, 1979), 110–134. Ovadiah was referred to as "the Norman" because he lived under Norman rule in southern Italy. On the case of Andreas, see Golb, "Jewish Proselytism," 10–12.

87. Alexander Scheiber, "The Origins of Obadya, the Norman Proselyte," in *The Legacy of Islamic Antisemitism*, 495–498.

88. For an analysis of this possibility, see Benjamin Z. Kedar, "The Voyages of Giuàn-Ovadiah in Syria and Iraq and the Enigma of His Conversion," in *Giovanni-Ovadiah da Oppido, proselito, viaggiatore e musicista dell'età normanna: atti del convegno internazionale, Oppido Lucano, 28–30 marzo 2004*, vol. 16, ed. Antonio de Rosa and Mauro Perani (Casa Editrice Giuntina, 2005), 141–147.

89. Golb, "Jewish Proselytism," 9–10.

90. See Paula Tartakoff, "Martyrdom, Conversion, and Shared Cultural Repertoires in Late Medieval Europe," *Jewish Quarterly Review* 109, no. 4 (2019): 500–503.

91. For a discussion of this topic see Tartakoff, "Martyrdom."

92. See Shlomo Simonsohn, *The Apostolic See and the Jews: History* (Pontifical Institute of Medieval Studies, 1991), 167–171. For a detailed description of early medieval royal and ecclesiastical legislation prohibiting Jewish slave ownership, see Bernhard Blumenkranz, *Juifs et Chrétiens dans le Monde Occidental, 430–1096* (Paris 1960), 184–209.

93. Simonsohn, *Apostolic See*, 232.

94. See Hillel Pinchas Halevi Applebaum, "Jewish Household Slaves in Medieval Ashkenaz" [Hebrew] (PhD diss., Bar-Ilan University, 2019), 160–161.

95. Grayzel, *Church and the Jews*, 23–24.

96. See David Berger, "Christians, Gentiles, and the Talmud: A Fourteenth-Century Jewish Response to the Attack on Rabbinic Judaism," in idem, *Persecution, Polemic, and Dialogue: Essays in Jewish-Christian Relations* (Academic Studies Press, 2010), 158–176; Robert Chazan, *Barcelona and Beyond: The Disputation of 1263 and Its Aftermath* (University of California Press, 1992).

97. See the conclusions of Robert Stacey for England in his essay, "The Conversion of Jews to Christianity in Thirteenth-Century England," *Speculum* 67, no. 2 (1992): 282–283.

98. See Tartakoff, *Between Christian and Jew*, 61–85; Stacey, "Conversion of Jews," 274–275.

99. See Paola Tartakoff, "Jewish Women and Apostasy in the Medieval Crown of Aragon," *Jewish History* 24 (2010): 7–32; Elisheva Carlebach, *Divided Souls: Converts from Judaism in Germany, 1500–1750* (Yale University Press, 2008), 138–156.

100. Tartakoff, "Jewish Women and Apostasy," 9.

101. Nicolas Donin was a key figure in the Paris trial of the Talmud in 1240, Pablo Christiani in the Disputation of Barcelona in 1263, and Jerónimo de Santa Fe in the Disputation of Tortosa in 1413–1414.

102. On the differing motivations of such figures see Jeremy Cohen, "The Mentality of the Medieval Jewish Apostate: Peter Alfonsi, Hermann of Cologne, and Pablo Christiani," in *Jewish Apostasy in the Modern World*, 20–47.

103. Ryan Szpiech, *Conversion and Narrative: Reading and Religious Authority in Medieval Polemic* (University of Pennsylvania Press, 2012), 5. In this work, Szpiech interprets conversion narratives that have often been taken at face value from the point of view of their symbolic and ideological functions. See also the detailed study of the twelfth-century narrative attributed to the former Jew Herman of Cologne by Jean-Claude Schmitt, *The Conversion of Herman the Jew: Autobiography, History, and Fiction in the Twelfth Century* (University of Pennsylvania Press, 2010).

104. See Tartakoff, *Between Christian and Jew*, 109–110; Edward Fram, "Perception and Reception of Repentant Apostates in Medieval Ashkenaz and Premodern Poland," *AJS Review* 21, no. 2 (1996): 299–339.

105. See David Malkiel, "Jews and Apostates in Medieval Europe—Boundaries Real and Imagined," *Past and Present* 194.1 (2007): 23–27; Stacey, "Conversion of Jews," 278–280.

106. The classic work on this principle is Jacob Katz, "'Even Though A Sinner, He Is Still of Israel'" [Hebrew], *Tarbiz* 27(1958), 203–27, and see idem, *Exclusiveness and Tolerance*, 67–81.

107. See Blidstein, "Who Is Not a Jew?" and Kanarfogel, *Brothers from Afar.*

108. Kanarfogel, *Brothers from Afar*, 31.

109. See Tartakoff, *Conversion, Circumcision*, 104–112.

110. See Kanarfogel, *Brothers from Afar*, 8–29.

111. See Yerushalmi, "The Inquisition and the Jews," 364.

112. On the practice of the immersion of returning apostates, see Ephraim Kanarfogel, "Returning to the Jewish Community in Medieval Ashkenaz: History and Halakhah," *Turim: Studies in Jewish History and Literature Presented to Dr. Bernard Lander* 1 (2007): 69–97; Tartakoff, *Between Christian and Jew*, 125–128.

113. The ritual that Bernard Gui described drew from at least one actual confession, and other sources mention similar "rejudaizing" practices. On these practices see Yerushalmi, "Inquisition and the Jews of France," 363–374.

114. Elsewhere, however, he declared that "we should not be so strict with him [the returnee], by requiring him to undergo afflictions in order to achieve expiation." See Kanarfogel, "Returning to the Jewish Community," 87–88, and Fram, "Perception and Reception," 304 n19.

115. Tartakoff, *Between Christian and Jew*, 2–3, 13–15, 101–104.

116. On the issues involved in labeling conversions "voluntary" or "forced" see Malkiel, "Jews and Apostates," 3–34.

117. Less well-known episodes are those in southern Italy in 1290–1293 and in southern France, with the Pastoureux uprising, in 1320–1321. On the first episode see Joshua Starr, "The Mass Conversion of Jews in Southern Italy (1290–1293)," *Speculum* 21, no. 2 (1946): 203–211; on the second, Yerushalmi, "Inquisition and the Jews of France," 328–333, and Tartakoff, *Between Christian and Jew*, 26–29.

118. Jeremy Cohen has argued that the Jewish glorification of martyrdom during and after the First Crusade mirrored the spiritual atmosphere of the Crusaders. See Jeremy Cohen, *Sanctifying the Name of God: Jewish Martyrs and Jewish Memories of the First Crusade* (University of Pennsylvania Press, 2013), 22–30.

119. Solomon Grayzel, *The Church and the Jews in the XIIIth Century II: 1254–1314*, edited by Kenneth Stow (New York: JTS, 1989), 103–104. For other cases in which forcibly converted Jews were allowed to return see Tartakoff, *Conversion, Circumcision*, 104.

120. See Malkiel, "Jews and Apostates," 19–20.

121. See the discussion of this church policy in Yerushalmi, "Inquisition and the Jews," 339–341. On this issue see also Jessie Sherwood, "Coacta voluntas est voluntas: Baptism and Return in Canon Law," *Medieval Encounters* 28, no. 6 (2022): 447–484.

122. On punishments of relapsed Jews and those who aided them see Fram, "Perception and Reception," 311–313.

123. See Tartakoff, *Conversion, Circumcision*, 118–119.

124. For a detailed account of the riots of 1391 in the Kingdom of Aragon, see Benjamin Gampel, *Anti-Jewish Riots in the Crown of Aragon and the Royal Response, 1391–1392* (Cambridge University Press, 2016).

CHAPTER 5 — EARLY MODERN

1. See Vera Moreen, "The Problems of Conversion Among Iranian Jews in the Seventeenth and Eighteenth Centuries," *Iranian Studies* 19, nos. 3–4 (1986): 215–228.

2. See Yaron Ben-Naeh, "Blond, Tall, with Honey-colored Eyes: Jewish Ownership of Slaves in the Ottoman Empire," *Jewish History* 20 (2006), 315–332.

3. See Marc David Baer, "Islamic Conversion Narratives of Women: Social Change and Gendered Religious Hierarchy in Early Modern Ottoman Istanbul," *Gender & History* 16, no. 2 (2004): 425–458.

4. Amnon Cohen and Elisheva Simon-Pikali, *Jews in the Moslem Religious Court: Society, Economy, and Communal Organization in the XVIth Century: Documents from Ottoman Jerusalem* (Yad Ben Zvi, 1993), 127–130; idem, *Jews in the Moslem Religious Court: Society, Economy, and Communal Organization in the XVIIth Century: Documents from Ottoman Jerusalem* (Yad Ben Zvi, 2010), 335–270; and see Amnon Cohen, *Jewish Life Under Islam: Jerusalem in the Sixteenth Century* (Harvard University Press, 1984), 73–76.

5. This is also the conclusion in a comparative study by Lea Bornstein Makovetsky, "Conversion to Islam in Ottoman Communities and to Christianity in Italy and Germany in the Sixteenth and Seventeenth Centuries" [Hebrew], *Peamim* 57 (1993): 29–47.

6. Elisheva Carlebach, *Divided Souls: Converts from Judaism in Germany, 1500–1750* (New Haven: Yale University Press, 2008), 88–123.

7. Carlebach, *Divided Souls*, 29.

8. See Ryan Szpiech, "From Convert to Convert: Two Opposed Trends in Late Medieval and Early Modern Anti-Jewish Polemic," in *Revealing the Secrets of the Jews: Johannes Pfefferkorn and Christian Writings About Jewish Life and Literature in Early Modern Europe*, ed. Cordelia Hess and Jonathan Adams (De Gruyter, 2017), 219–243.

9. On this literature see Carlebach, *Divided Souls*, 170–199.

10. On apostates in these roles see Carlebach, *Divided Souls*, 200–221. On Christian Hebraists see Steven Burnett, *Christian Hebraism in the Reformation Era (1500–1600)* (Brill, 2012); Allison Coudert and Jeffrey Shoulson, eds., *Hebraica veritas? Christian Hebraists and the Study of Judaism in Early Modern Europe* (University of Pennsylvania Press, 2004).

11. A vivid case in point is that of the Helicz brothers in sixteenth-century Cracow. See Magda Teter and Edward Fram, "Apostasy, Fraud, and the Beginnings of Hebrew Printing in Cracow," *AJS Review* 30, no. 1 (2006): 31–66.

12. Among such converts were the Italian Giovanni Laurento di Buongiorno, Simon Pecs in Transylvania, the Frenchman Nicolas Antoine, Benedictus Sperling in

Altona, Johann Peter Späth from Germany, and the Frenchman Aaron d'Anton. For references, see Miriam Bodian, *Dying in the Law of Moses: Crypto-Jewish Martyrdom in the Iberian world* (Indiana University Press, 2007), 248 n.4–9.

13. See Allison Coudert, "Judaizing in the Seventeenth Century: Francis Mercury van Helmont and Johann Peter Späth (Moses Germanus)," in *Secret Conversions to Judaism in Early Modern Europe,* ed. Martin Mulsow and Richard H. Popkin (Brill, 2004), 74.

14. On Späth, see Allison Coudert, "Judaizing," 71–121; on d'Antan see Martin Mulsow, "Cartesianism, Skepticism and Conversion to Judaism: The Case of Aaron d'Antan," in *Secret Conversions,* 123–181.

15. For discussion of a controversy involving Gentile converts to Judaism in Hoorn in 1615, see Alexander van der Haven, "Conversion on Trial: Toleration of Apostasy and the Trial of Three Converts to Judaism in the Dutch Republic, 1614–1615," in *Contesting Inter-Religious Conversion in the Medieval World,* ed. Yosi Yisraeli and Yaniv Fox (Routledge, 2017), 49–68. See also Yosef Kaplan, "Proselytes and Conversion to Judaism in the Early Modern Sephardi Community of Amsterdam," in *Et amicorum: estudios en honor al Profesor Carlos Carrete Parrondo,* ed. Efrem Yildiz (Ediciones Universidad Salamanca, 2019), 379–386. On Amsterdam as a haven for "returning" baptized German Jews, see Elisheva Carlebach, "'Ich will dich nach Holland schicken . . .': Amsterdam and the Reversion to Judaism of German-Jewish Converts," in *Secret Conversions,* 51–69.

16. On the conversion of convicted Jewish criminals, see Tamar Herzig, "The Coerced Conversion of Convicted Jewish Criminals in Fifteenth-Century Italy," in *Forced Conversion in Christianity, Judaism and Islam: Coercion and Faith in Premodern Iberia and Beyond,* ed. Mercedes García-Arenal and Yonatan Glazer-Eytan (Brill, 2020), 266–288, and Tamar Herzig, *A Convert's Tale: Art, Crime, and Jewish Apostasy in Renaissance Italy* (Harvard University Press, 2019).

17. On the houses of catechumens see Peter Mazur, *Conversion to Catholicism in Early Modern Italy* (Routledge, 2016), 18–42.

18. On the tangled career of Flavius Mithridates, a Renaissance Jew-turned-Italian humanist, as well as later Catholic Reformation converts who engaged in anti-Jewish polemics, see Shlomo Simonsohn, "Some Well-Known Jewish Converts During the Renaissance," *Revue des études juives* 148 (1989), 20–38. See also Mazur, *Conversion,* 66–76.

19. On the return of the baptized Jews, see Fram, "Perception and Reception of Repentant Apostates," 322.

20. On the conversion efforts of the Jesuits, see Magdalena Teter, "Jewish Conversions to Catholicism in the Polish-Lithuanian Commonwealth of the Seventeenth and Eighteenth Centuries," *Jewish History* 17, no. 3 (2003): 257–283.

21. On the terminology applied to this population see Yosi Yisraeli and Yanay Israeli, "Defining 'Conversos' in Fifteenth-Century Castile: The Making of a Controversial Category," *Speculum* 97, no. 3 (2022): 609–648.

22. The classic elucidation of the reasons is found in Yosef Hayim Yerushalmi, *From Spanish Court to Italian Ghetto: Isaac Cardoso—A Study in Seventeenth-Century Marranism and Jewish Apologetics* (University of Washington Press, 1981), 4–8.

23. On the early modern Iberian conceptualization of Jewish "blood," see David Nirenberg, "Was There Race Before Modernity? The Example of 'Jewish' Blood in Late Medieval Spain," in *The Origins of Racism in the West*, ed. Miriam Eliav-Feldon et al. (Cambridge University Press, 2009), 239–264.

24. For one inquisitor's view that nothing short of a miracle was required to bring about the true conversion of a person with Jewish ancestry, see Miriam Bodian, "Behind Closed Doors: A Dominican Friar's 'Debate' with a Dutch Jew, from the Records of an Inquisition Trial, Lisbon, 1645–1666," *Jewish Studies Quarterly* 21, no. 4 (2014): 376–387. Doubts about the efficacy of baptism in cases of Jewish conversions were sometimes raised outside Iberian lands as well; see Carlebach, *Divided Souls*, 35–37.

25. For a discussion of the nature of this "forgetting" see Miriam Bodian, *Dying in the Law*, 37–38.

26. On rabbinic responsa dealing with these issues, see Yerushalmi, *From Spanish Court*, 24–31.

27. See Claude Stuczynski, "Harmonizing Identities: The Problem of the Integration of the Portuguese Conversos in Early Modern Iberian Corporate Polities," *Jewish History* 25, no. 2 (2011): 229–257.

28. For some cases of this, see David Gitlitz, *Secrecy and Deceit: The Religion of the Crypto-Jews* (Jewish Publication Society, 1996), 564–569.

29. On Molkho, see Zvi Werblowsky, "R. R. Joseph Caro, Solomon Molcho, Don Joseph Nasi," in *Moreshet Sepharad: The Sephardi Legacy*, 2 vols., ed. Haim Beinart (Magnes Press, 1992), 2:179–191.

30. See Bodian, *Dying in the Law*, esp. 36, 52–53, 126.

31. Bodian, *Dying in the Law*, 169–171.

32. On the memorialization of these figures in Amsterdam, see Bodian, *Dying in the Law*, 179–180.

33. See Bodian, *Dying in the Law*.

34. Renée Levine Melammed, *Heretics or Daughters of Israel? The Crypto-Jewish Women of Castile* (Oxford University Press, 1999), 168.

35. This was articulated by the seventeenth-century Venetian rabbi Samuel Aboab. Aboab defined as apostates only those persons who "had previously been [unbaptized]

Jews, who understood the nature of the Jewish tradition." Their descendants, however, who did not know that tradition, he defined as "infants taken captive among the Gentiles." Miriam Bodian, *Hebrews of the Portuguese Nation: Conversos and Community in Early Modern Amsterdam* (Indiana University Press, 1997), 138.

36. Yosef Kaplan, "'This Thing Alone Will Preserve Their Nation Forever': Circumcision and Conversion in the Early Modern Western Sephardic Communities," in *The Conversos and Moriscos in Late Medieval Spain and Beyond*, ed. Kevin Ingram and J. I. Pulido Serrano (Brill, 2016), 230n35.

37. The importance of this specific precept was underscored by the practice of depriving males who resisted circumcision of full participation in communal life. See Kaplan, "This Thing Alone," 231–235.

38. This is vividly expressed in the description that the ex-converso Isaac de Pinto gave of his own experience after arriving in the Netherlands. See Bodian, *Hebrews*, 96.

39. On the identification with the Israelites in Egypt, see Bodian, *Hebrews*, 15, 40.

40. See Anne Oravetz Albert, "Return by Any Other Name: Religious Change Among Amsterdam's New Jews," in *Bastards and Believers*, 140–145.

41. Daniel Levi de Barrios, "Carça de Mosseh," in *Triumpho del govierno popular, y de la antiguedad Holandesa* (Amsterdam, 1683–1685). My translation. My thanks to Anne Oravetz Albert for providing me with the original Spanish text. Cited in Albert, "Return by Any Other Name," 134.

42. See Bodian, *Dying in the Law*; Miriam Bodian, "The Geography of Conscience: A Seventeenth-Century Atlantic Jew and the Inquisition," *Journal of Modern History* 89, no. 2 (2017): 247–281; Carsten Wilke, "Conversion ou retour? La métamorphose du nouveau chrétien en juif Portugais dans l'imaginaire sépharade du XVIIe siècle," in *Mémoires juives d'Espagne et du Portugal*, ed. Esther Benbassa (Publisud, 1996), 53–77; idem, "Conversion Theology Among Sixteenth-Century Portuguese Jews: Protestant and Islamic Subtexts," in *In the Iberian Peninsula and Beyond: A History of Jews and Muslims (15th–17th Centuries)*, vol. 1, ed. Maria Filomena Lopes de Barros et al. (Cambridge Scholars Publishing, 2015), 252–265. In the latter, Wilke contrasts the collective representation of conversion in Samuel Usque's *Consolation for the Tribulations of Israel* (Ferrara, 1553) with the individual spiritual transformation represented in the *Marrakesh Dialogues*, in which he argues, "The movement of return was re-imagined as a form of Jewish proselytism." Carsten Wilke, *The Marrakesh Dialogues: A Gospel Critique and Jewish Apology from the Spanish Renaissance* (Brill 2014), 9.

43. See Miriam Bodian, "Uriel da Costa's Career: An Interpretation," in *From Doubt to Unbelief: Forms of Scepticism in the Iberian World*, ed. Mercedes García-Arenal and Stefania Pastore (Legenda, 2019), 239–267.

44. On ex-conversos who led such double lives see Brian Pullan, "'A Ship with Two Rudders':'Righetto Marrano' and the Inquisition in Venice," *Historical Journal* 20, no. 1 (1977): 25–58; Yosef Kaplan, "Amsterdam, the Forbidden Lands, and the Dynamics of the Sephardi Diaspora," in idem, *The Dutch Intersection: The Jews and the Netherlands in Modern History* (Brill, 2008), 33–62; David Graizbord, *Souls in Dispute: Converso Identities in Iberia and the Jewish Diaspora* (University of Pennsylvania Press, 2013).

45. Isaac Orobio de Castro, *Respuesta a un Cavallero Francés*, Ets Haim Ms. 48D6, 307v.

46. See Kaplan, "Proselytes and Conversion," 379–388.

47. See Makovetsky, "Conversion to Islam," 29–47.

48. See Baer, "Islamic Conversion Narratives of Women," 425–458.

49. The classic account of Shabbetai Zevi's apostasy is Gershom Scholem, *Sabbatai Sevi: The Mystical Messiah* (Princeton University Press, 1973), 673–681.

50. See Marc David Baer, *Honored by the Glory of Islam: Conversion and Conquest in Ottoman Europe* (Oxford University Press, 2008), 121–138.

51. On the aftermath of Sabbatai's apostasy see Scholem, *Sabbatai Sevi*, 687–820.

52. On the Dönmeh see Marc David Baer, *The Dönme: Jewish Converts, Muslim Revolutionaries, and Secular Turks* (Stanford University Press, 2010); Cengiz Sisman, *The Burden of Silence: Sabbatai Sevi and the Evolution of the Ottoman-Turkish Dönmes* (Oxford University Press, 2015).

53. See Paweł Maciejko, *The Mixed Multitude: Jacob Frank and the Frankist Movement, 1755–1816* (University of Pennsylvania Press, 2011).

CHAPTER 6 — MODERN

1. Jonathan Helfand, "Passports and Piety: Apostasy in Nineteenth-Century France," *Jewish History* 3 (1988): 59.

2. For a detailed discussion see Deborah Hertz, "Seductive Conversion in Berlin, 1770–1809," in *Jewish Apostasy in the Modern World*, ed. Todd Endelman (Holmes & Meier, 1987), 48–82.

3. On the crisis of the late eighteenth and early nineteenth centuries see Steven Lowenstein, *The Berlin Jewish Community: Enlightenment, Family and Crisis, 1770–1830* (Oxford University Press, 1994), 95–103.

4. See Steven Lowenstein, "Reflections on Statistics: Hopes and Fears About Changes in the German Jewish Family, 1815–1939," *Leo Baeck Institute Yearbook* 51 (2006): 57–59.

5. *Shulkhan Arukh, Yoreh De'ah* 268.

6. David Ellenson, "The Orthodox Rabbinate and Apostasy in Nineteenth-Century Germany and Hungary," in Endelman, *Jewish Apostasy*, 170.

7. See the analysis in Avi Sagi and Zvi Zohar, *Transforming Identity: The Ritual Transformation from Gentile to Jew—Structure and Meaning* (Continuum, 2009), 40. The responsum in question was published in 1860.

8. For an analysis of the different Orthodox approaches to this issue see Sagi and Zohar, *Transforming Identity*, 37–103, 223–251; David Ellenson and Daniel Gordis, *Pledges of Jewish Allegiance: Conversion, Law, and Policymaking in Nineteenth-and Twentieth-Century Orthodox Responsa* (Stanford University Press, 2012).

9. Ismar Schorsch, "Moritz Güdemann: Rabbi, Historian and Apologist," *Leo Baeck Institute Yearbook* 11, no. 1 (1966): 46.

10. For an example, see Dana Evan Kaplan, "Intermarriage and Conversion to Judaism in Early American Orthodoxy," *Tradition: A Journal of Orthodox Jewish Thought* 31, no. 4 (1997): 41–42.

11. See Kaplan, "Intermarriage and Conversion," 47.

12. Michael Meyer, "New Water in an Old Vessel: A History of Mikveh in Modern Judaism," in *Between Jewish Tradition and Modernity: Rethinking an Old Opposition*, ed. Michael Meyer and David Myers (Wayne State University Press, 2014), 145.

13. See David Novak, "The Status of Non-Halakhic Conversions," *Proceedings of the Committee on Jewish Law and Standards I 1980–1985*, 78. https://www.rabbinicalassembly.org/sites/default/files/assets/public/halakhah/teshuvot/20012004/16.pdf.

14. See Novak, "Status of Non-Halakhic Conversions"; Joel Roth, "Should the Kashrut of Conversions Be Investigated?" *Proceedings of the Committee on Jewish Law and Standards I 1980–1985*, https://www.rabbinicalassembly.org/sites/default/files/assets/public/halakhah/teshuvot/20012004/17.pdf.

15. For a Conservative perspective, see Roth, "Should the Kashrut of Conversions."

16. Moshe Yeres, "Burial of Non-Halakhic Converts," *Tradition: A Journal of Orthodox Jewish Thought* 23, no. 3 (1988): 60–74.

17. See Alan Levenson, "Reform Attitudes in the Past Toward Intermarriage," *Judaism* 38, no. 3 (1989): 330–332.

18. See Dana Evan Kaplan, "W. E. Todd's Attempt to Convert to Judaism and Study for the Reform Rabbinate in 1896," *American Jewish History* 83, no. 4 (1995): 429–444; quote on 438.

19. On Gordon's career see Marsha Keith Schuchard, "Lord George Gordon and Cabalistic Freemasonry: Beating Jacobite Swords into Jacobin Ploughshares," in *Secret Conversions to Judaism in Early Modern Europe*, 183–231; Jeffrey Spear, "Of Jews and Ships and Mob Attacks, of Catholics and Kings: The Curious Career of Lord George Gordon," *Dickens Studies Annual* 31 (2002): 65–106; Israel Solomons, "Lord George Gordon's Conversion to Judaism," *Transactions of the Jewish Historical Society of England* 7 (1911): 222–271.

20. On Cresson, see Frank Fox, "Quaker, Shaker, Rabbi: Warder Cresson, the Story of a Philadelphia Mystic," *Pennsylvania Magazine of History and Biography* (1971): 147–194. On his agricultural settlement see Ruth Kark, "Millenarism and Agricultural Settlement in the Holy Land in the Nineteenth Century," *Journal of Historical Geography* 9, no. 1 (1983): 50–53.

21. Endelman, "Introduction," in Endelman, *Jewish Apostasy*, 10, 18–19 n6.

22. On the phenomenon of Jewish "passing" see Todd Endelman, *Leaving the Jewish Fold: Conversion and Radical Assimilation in Modern Jewish History* (Princeton University Press, 2015), 172–189.

23. Endelman, *Leaving the Fold*.

24. Adam Ferziger, "From Demonic Deviant to Drowning Brother: Reform Judaism in the Eyes of American Orthodoxy," *Jewish Social Studies: History, Culture, and Society* 15, no. 3 (2009): 58.

25. Ellenson, "Orthodox Rabbinate," in Endelman, *Jewish Apostasy*, 169–173.

26. Ellenson, "Orthodox Rabbinate," in Endelman, *Jewish Apostasy*, 171–183.

27. For examples see Endelman, *Leaving the Fold*, 350–353.

28. See Endelman, *Leaving the Fold*, 118.

29. Gershom Scholem, *From Berlin to Jerusalem* (Schocken, 1980), 11.

30. Sholem Aleichem, *Tevye the Dairyman and the Railroad Stories*, trans. Hillel Halkin (Schocken, 2011), 80.

31. Todd Endelman, "The Social and Political Context of Conversion in Germany and England, 1870–1914," in Endelman, *Jewish Apostasy*, 87–93.

32. See Ellie Schainker, *Confessions of the Shtetl: Converts from Judaism in Imperial Russia, 1817–1906* (Stanford University Press, 2016), 85–100.

33. See Todd Endelman, "Gender and Conversion Revisited," in *Gender and Jewish History*, ed. Marion Kaplan and Deborah Dash Moore (Indiana University Press, 2011), 170–172.

34. Deborah Hertz, "Emancipation Through Intermarriage in Old Berlin," in *Jewish Women in Historical Perspective*, ed. Judith Baskin (Wayne State University Press, 1991), 198.

35. Endelman, "Gender and Conversion," 174.

36. Endelman, "Gender and Conversion."

37. On the gendered nature of conversion in late nineteenth-century Galicia, see Rachel Manekin, *The Rebellion of the Daughters: Jewish Women Runaways in Habsburg Galicia* (Princeton University Press, 2020) and "The Lost Generation: Education and Female Conversion in Fin-de-Siècle Kraków," *Polin* 18 (2005): 189–219.

38. Endelman, "Gender and Conversion," 184.

39. See Endelman, *Leaving the Fold*, 228–237. For the passage dealing with Alphonse Ratisbonne, see William James, *The Varieties of Religious Experience: A Study in Human Nature* (Longmans, Green and Co., 1917), 223–226.

40. Endelman, *Leaving the Fold*, 76–78, 247–250.

41. Endelman, *Leaving the Fold*, 113–117, 152–161; William McCagg, "Jewish Conversion in Hungary in Modern Times," in Endelman, *Jewish Apostasy*, 157–159.

42. Endelman, *Leaving the Fold*, 192–201.

43. See Olga Litvak, *Conscription and the Search for Modern Russian Jewry* (Indiana University Press, 2006), 28, 214–215, n52.

44. Schainker, *Confessions of the Shtetl*, 67.

45. David Kertzer, *The Kidnapping of Edgardo Mortara* (Knopf, 1997).

46. On other episodes see David Kertzer, *The Popes Against the Jews: The Vatican's Role in the Rise of Modern Anti-Semitism* (Vintage, 2007), 38–59.

47. See Bat-Zion Eraqi Klorman's study of Jewish apostasy in Yemen, "Muslim Society as an Alternative: Jews Converting to Islam," *Jewish Social Studies* 14 (2007): 89–99.

48. Klorman, "Muslim Society," 101–102.

49. For Yemen, see Klorman, "Muslim Society"; for Turkey and the Balkans see Leah Bornstein-Makovetsky, "Jewish Converts to Islam and Christianity in the Ottoman Empire in the Nineteenth Century," in *The Last Ottoman Century and Beyond: The Jews in Turkey and the Balkans*, ed. Minna Rozen (Goldstein-Goren Diaspora Research Center, 2002), 2: 83–127; for Iraq, see Nissim Kazzaz, "Conversions Among the Jews of Iraq in Modern Times" [Hebrew], *Peamim* 42 (1990), 157–158.

50. Kazzaz, "Conversions Among Jews of Iraq," 157–165.

51. Hilda Nissimi, *The Crypto-Jewish Mashhadis: The Shaping of Religious and Communal Identity in Their Journey from Iran to New York* (Liverpool University Press, 2006); Ariane Sadjed, "Conversion, Identity, and Memory in Iranian-Jewish Historiography: The Jews of Mashhad," *International Journal of Middle East Studies* 53, no. 2 (2021): 235–251.

CHAPTER 7 — STATE OF ISRAEL

1. On Ben-Gurion's views, see Netanel Fisher and Avi Shilon, "Integrating Non-Jewish Immigrants and the Formation of Israel's Ethnic–Civic Nationhood: From Ben-Gurion to the Present," *Middle Eastern Studies* 53, no. 2 (2017): 172–174.

2. Nicole Maor and David Ellenson, "'Who Is a Convert?'—The Law of Return and the Legality of Reform and Conservative Conversions in Israel," *Israel Studies* 27, no. 2 (2022): 26.

3. On this case see, Maor and Ellenson, "Who is a Convert?" 26–27.

4. Maor and Ellenson, "Who is a Convert?" 28–29.

5. Netanel Fisher, "Introduction to the History of Conversion in the IDF" [Hebrew], in *Safra v-Saifa—Jubilee Book in Honor of Rabbi Mordechai Piron*, ed. Zvi Tal, Aviad HaCohen, and Hananel Mack (Sapir Institute, 2013), 413–429.

6. Shlomo Goren, *Mishnat ha-medinah: Meḥḳar hilkhati hisṭori ba-nośʼim ha-ʻomdim be-rumah shel medinat Yiśraʼel me-az teḳumatah* (Hotsaʼat ha-Idra rabah u-mesorah la-ʻam, 1998/1999), 181–185.

7. Netanel Fisher, "A Jewish State? Controversial Conversions and the Dispute over Israel's Jewish Character," *Contemporary Jewry* 33 (2013): 228–229; Goren, *Mishnat ha-medinah*, 184–185.

8. See Goren, *Mishnat ha-medinah*, 186–190.

9. Netanel Fisher, "'Israeli' Halakha: The Chief Rabbinate's Conversion-to-Judaism Policy 1948–2018," *Modern Judaism* 39, no. 1 (2019): 77.

10. Ruth Gavison, "The Law of Return at Sixty Years: History, Ideology, Justification," 2010. http://dx.doi.org/10.2139/ssrn.1951784.

11. A slight qualification: Small numbers of Russian-Jewish emigres, both in Israel and the diaspora, have been baptized in the Russian Orthodox Church and identify as both Jewish and Christian. See Judith Deutsch Kornblatt, *Doubly Chosen: Jewish Identity, the Soviet Intelligentsia, and the Russian Orthodox Church* (University of Wisconsin Press, 2004).

12. Michal Kravel-Tovi, *When the State Winks: The Performance of Jewish Conversion in Israel* (Columbia University Press, 2018), 73; see the discussion on pp. 72–76.

13. Arie Haskin, "Non-Jewish Immigrants from the FSU as Members of Jewish Society in Israel," in *Becoming Jewish: New Jews and Emerging Jewish Communities in a Globalized World*, ed. Tudor Parfitt and Netanel Fisher (Cambridge University Press, 2016), 251.

14. See Anna Prashizky and Larissa Remennick, "Gender and Cultural Citizenship Among Non-Jewish Immigrants from the Former Soviet Union in Israel," *Citizenship Studies* 18, no. 3–4 (2014): 380.

15. For an ethnographic study of conversion under this program see Kravel-Tovi, *When the State Winks*.

16. Kravel-Tovi, *When the State Winks*, 78.

17. See Kravel-Tovi, *When the State Winks*.

18. See the data in Fisher, "'Israeli' Halakha," 98.

19. Conversation with Shaul Farber, May 15, 2023.

20. On the efforts of the state conversion authority see Kravel-Tovi, *When the State Winks*, 78–84.

21. Gavison, "Law of Return," 84.

22. See Haskin, "Non-Jewish Immigrants from the FSU," in *Becoming Jewish*, 248.

23. Regev Ben-David, "Your People Shall Be My People and Your Culture My Culture': Becoming a Jew—A Peoplehood Perspective," in *Becoming Jewish*, 293–312.

24. According to a leading halakhic expert on conversion, the possibility of annulling a conversion appeared in the halakhic literature only in the nineteenth century. See Menachem Finkelstein, *Conversion: Halakhah and Practice* (Bar-Ilan University Press, 2006), 620.

25. Kravel-Tovi, *When the State Winked*, 122.

CHAPTER 8 — UNITED STATES

1. This is not to minimize real differences among diaspora populations. Especially in postwar Germany and Poland, for example, strong identification with Jewish suffering and the destruction of Jewish culture during the Holocaust motivated a significant number of conversions to Judaism. See Barbara Steiner, "The German Desire to Be Jewish: Conversions of Non-Jewish Germans to Judaism After 1945," in *Becoming Jewish: New Jews and Emerging Jewish Communities in a Globalized World*, ed. Tudor Parfitt and Netanel Fisher (Cambridge University Press, 2016), 156–166; Jan Lorenz, "Polish Newcomers to Jewishness: A Reflection in the Wake of the Revival," in *Becoming Jewish*, 167–184.

2. David Max Eichhorn, "Conversions to Judaism by Reform and Conservative Rabbis," *Jewish Social Studies* 16 (1954): 310, 301–322. The survey did not cover Orthodox conversions.

3. See https://www.jta.org/2015/07/06/culture/10-interesting-things-about-the-rcas-report-on-conversion-reform.

4. According to data from a population survey, from 1970 to 1990 12 percent of non-Jewish women and 5 percent of non-Jewish men who married Jews converted to Judaism; as of 1990, the overall figure was about 16 percent. Sylvia Barack Fishman, *Choosing Jewish: Conversations About Conversion* (American Jewish Committee, 2006), 114 n2.

5. Egon Mayer and Amy Avgar, *Conversion Among the Intermarried: Choosing to Become Jewish* (American Jewish Committee, 1987).

6. Fishman, *Choosing Jewish*, 3.

7. On the impact of American consumer mentality on the behavior model adopted by clergy, see Robert Wuthnow, *America and the Challenges of Religious Diversity* (Princeton University Press, 2005), 266–271.

8. The participating rabbis who identified as modern Orthodox were associated with "Traditional" synagogues, which deviated from Orthodox practice in several respects.

9. On the Denver initiative, see Dana Kaplan, *Contemporary American Judaism: Transformation and Renewal* (Columbia University Press, 2011), 191–195.

10. See Moshe Zemer, "The Rabbinic Ban on Conversion in Argentina," *Judaism* 37, no. 1 (1988): 84–96.

11. See Richard Hidary, "Sephardic Approaches to Conversion," in *Conversion, Intermarriage, and Jewish Identity*, ed. Adam Mintz and Marc Stern (Ktav, 2015), 314–318.

12. On Black converts to Judaism see the sociological study of Bruce Haynes, *The Soul of Judaism: Jews of African Descent in America* (New York University Press, 2018), esp. 111–140.

13. Nicole Bauer, "The Kabbalah Centre and Spirituality of the Self," *International Journal for the Study of New Religions* 10, no. 1 (2019): 50.

14. For a discussion of the commodified American "spiritual marketplace" see Wuthnow, *America and the Challenges*, 106–130.

15. On Schachter-Shalomi's thinking about conversion see Shaul Magid, *American Post-Judaism: Identity and Renewal in a Postethnic Society* (Indiana University Press, 2013), 48–56.

16. Although the ideological approbation of a multitraditional religious identity may be new, the phenomenon is not. Arthur Nock, in his seminal work on conversion, referred to commitment to a new tradition without relinquishing the old as "adhesion," in contradistinction to "conversion." See Arthur Nock, *Conversion: The Old and the New in Religion from Alexander the Great to Augustine of Hippo* (Oxford University Press, 1933), 7.

17. See https://urj.org/blog/numerous-stars-heaven.

18. See https://darshanyeshiva.org/about-us/.

19. See https://simshalom.com/jewish-conversion/.

20. See https://www.ritualwell.org/jewish-conversion-101.

21. See, inter alia, Dory Fox, "Jewish Genetic Potency: The Meaning of Jewish Ancestry in the 21st-Century United States," *American Jewish History* 104, no. 1 (2020): 59–86.

CHAPTER 9 — "EMERGING JEWS"

1. See Itzhak Ben-Zvi's *The Exiled and the Redeemed* (Jewish Publication Society, 1957) for a sense of his sweeping embrace of "other" Jews. The many problems with Ben-Zvi's representation are obvious today but should not detract from his role in bringing attention to marginalized Jews and groups that claimed Jewish descent.

2. On the Mashhadi Jews, see Raphael Patai, *Jadīd Al-Islām: The Jewish "New Muslims" of Meshhed* (Wayne State University Press, 1997); Ariane Sadjed, "Conversion, Identity, and Memory in Iranian-Jewish Historiography: The Jews of Mashhad," *International Journal of Middle East Studies* 53, no. 2 (2021): 235–251. On the deliberations about the Mashhadi Jews' status see Patai, *Jadīd Al-Islām*, 110–111.

3. On the Belmonte Jews see Naomi Leite, *Unorthodox Kin: Portuguese Marranos and the Global Search for Belonging* (University of California Press, 2017), index. Although the book's focus is not on the rural Belmonte Jews, it deals with them in some depth and is one of the few studies that does so in a scholarly fashion.

4. On this phenomenon, see the various studies by Tudor Parfitt, Emanuela Trevisan Semi, Shalva Weil, and Yulia Egorova. In a more popular vein, see Hillel Halkin, *Across the Sabbath River: In Search of a Lost Tribe of Israel* (Houghton Mifflin, 2002).

5. On the Lemba, see the ethnographic study of Noah Tamarkin, *Genetic Afterlives: Black Jewish Indigeneity in South Africa* (Duke University Press, 2020).

6. On the recently emerging urban "Marranos" in Portugal (not to be confused with the Belmonte and other rural Jews) see Leite, *Unorthodox Kin*.

7. On these groups see Jacob Dorman, *Chosen People: The Rise of American Black Israelite Religions* (Oxford University Press, 2012); Judith Weisenfeld, *New World A-Coming: Black Religion and Racial Identity During the Great Migration* (New York University Press, 2017). On the issues around the status of Black Israelites who have settled in Israel, see the tendentious but informative Fran Markowitz, Sara Helman, and Dafna Shir-Vertesh, "Soul Citizenship: The Black Hebrews and the State of Israel," *American Anthropologist* 105, no. 2 (2003): 302–312.

8. Figures from the Israel Central Bureau of Statistics show that at the end of 2022, residents of Ethiopian origin in Israel numbered 168,800.

9. For English translations of the two responsa, see Michael Corinaldi, *Jewish Identity: The Case of Ethiopian Jewry* (Magnes Press, 1998), 189–196. On Radbaz's leniency concerning marriage see Corinaldi, *Jewish Identity*, 104–105.

10. On European Protestant interest in the "Falashas," see Daniel Summerfield, *From Falashas to Ethiopian Jews: The External Influences for Change c. 1860–1960* (Routledge, 2003), 3–34.

11. On the various programs conducted by foreign entities see Summerfield, *From Falashas*, 34–128.

12. On the successive waves of immigration in these years, see Steven Kaplan and Chaim Rosen, "Ethiopian Jews in Israel," *American Jewish Year Book* 94 (1994): 59–109.

13. This entailed symbolic ritual circumcision for the men *(hatafat dam)*, immersion without a benediction, and verbal acceptance of halakha.

14. Most importantly, the rabbinate recognized the validity of Beta Israel traditional circumcisions and did not require *hatafat dam*.

15. For a synopsis of this rather complex set of developments see Corinaldi, *Jewish Identity*, 115–119.

16. See Shalva Weil, "The Complexities of Conversion Among the 'Felesmura,'" in *Movements in Ethiopia, Ethiopia in Movement, vol.* 1, ed. Éloi Ficquet, Ahmed Hassen

Omer, and Thomas Osmond (Tsehai Publishers, 2016), 427; Don Seeman, *One People, One Blood: Ethiopian-Israelis and the Return to Judaism* (Rutgers University Press, 2009).

17. Missionaries sometimes came to believe they were hastening the millennium by "saving" remote peoples they identified with the Lost Tribes.

18. On the Bnei Menashe, see Shalva Weil, "Lost Israelites from the Indo-Burmese Borderlands: Re-Traditionalisation and Conversion Among the Shinlung or Bene Menasseh," *The Anthropologist* 6, no. 3 (2004): 219–233; Yulia Egorova, "Redefining the Converted Jewish Self: Race, Religion, and Israel's Bene Menashe," *American Anthropologist* 117, no. 3 (2015): 493–505.

19. See Graciela Mochkofsky, *The Prophet of the Andes: An Unlikely Journey to the Promised Land* (Alfred Knopf, 2022).

20. See John Davis, *The Jews of San Nicandro* (Yale University Press, 2010).

CHAPTER 10 — THINKING ABOUT JEWISH CONVERSION IN THE TWENTY-FIRST CENTURY

1. Jacob Katz, *Exclusiveness and Tolerance* (Behrman House, 1961), 67–76.

2. See especially the studies of Paola Tartakoff, David Malkiel, and Elisheva Carlebach cited in previous chapters, as well as Jeremy Cohen, "Between Martyrdom and Apostasy: Doubt and Self-Definition in Twelfth-Century Ashkenaz," *Journal of Medieval and Early Modern Studies* 29, no. 3 (1999): 431–471.

3. On the reversion of baptized Jews, see Ephraim Kanarfogel, *Brothers from Afar: Rabbinic Approaches to Apostasy and Reversion in Medieval Europe* (Wayne State University Press, 2020).

4. See Todd Endelman, *Leaving the Jewish Fold* (Princeton University Press, 2015).

5. *Handbook of Leaving Religion*, ed. Daniel Enstedt, Göran Larsson, and Teemu T. Mantsinen (Brill, 2020), 1–7. Under the rubric "leaving religion," the editors include leaving religion altogether and the abandonment of one faith community for another. In this book I used the term "apostasy" because it has no useful alternative in English and, despite its negative connotations, can simply mean, as Merriam-Webster has it, "an act of refusing to continue to follow, obey, or recognize a religious faith."

6. For two important efforts to define the field, see *Oxford Handbook of Religious Conversion*, ed. Lewis Rambo and Charles Farhadian (Oxford University Press, 2014); *Religious Conversion: History, Experience, and Meaning*, ed. Ira Katznelson and Miri Rubin (Routledge, 2014). For a list of publications attesting to the growth of this field in the first decade and a half of the twenty-first century, see *Contesting Inter-Religious Conversion in the Medieval World*, ed. Yosi Yisraeli and Yaniv Fox (Routledge, 2019), 16 n3.

7. An exception is Leora Batnitzky, "Between Ancestry and Belief: 'Judaism' and 'Hinduism' in the Nineteenth Century," *Modern Judaism* 41, no. 2 (2021): 194–219, in which the author discusses the way in which Jews and Hindus in a nineteenth-century

colonial context similarly insisted on the validity of ancestry and national identity as elements in conversion, as against a Christian conception of conversion that denied their relevance.

8. See Katznelson and Rubin, *Religious Conversion*; Yisraeli and Fox, *Contesting Inter-Religious Conversion*; *Forced Conversion*, ed. Mercedes García-Arenal and Yonatan Glazer-Eytan (Brill, 2019); and *Cultural and Religious Boundary-Crossing in Early Modern Spain*, ed. Miriam Bodian (Springer, 2022).

9. James Amelang, *Parallel Histories: Muslims and Jews in Inquisitorial Spain* (Louisiana State University Press, 2013). For other comparative studies of these populations, see Natalia Muchnik, "At the Crossroads of Identity: Conversos and Moriscos in Inquisitorial Spain (Sixteenth and Seventeenth Centuries)," in *Early Modern Toleration: New Approaches*, ed. Benjamin Kaplan and Jaap Geraerts (Routledge, 2024), 91–107; Renée Levine Melammed, "Judeo-Conversas and Moriscas in Sixteenth-Century Spain: A Study of Parallels," *Jewish History* 24, no. 2 (2010): 155–168.

10. On this tension see Christine Hayes, "The Complicated Goy in Classical Rabbinic Sources," in *Perceiving the Other in Ancient Judaism and Early Christianity*, ed. Michal Bar-Asher Siegal, Wolfgang Grünstäudl, and Matthew Thiessen (Mohr Siebeck, 2017), 147–67.

11. Shaye Cohen, *The Beginnings of Jewishness: Boundaries, Varieties, Uncertainties* (University of California Press, 1999), 5, 3.

12. For a seminal description of this shift see Cohen, *Beginnings of Jewishness*, 109–139.

13. See Christine Hayes, *Gentile Impurities and Jewish Identities: Intermarriage and Conversion from the Bible to the Talmud* (Oxford University Press, 2002).

14. See, inter alia, Matthew Thiessen, *Contesting Conversion: Genealogy, Circumcision, and Identity in Ancient Judaism and Christianity* (Oxford University Press, 2011); Moshe Lavee, *The Rabbinic Conversion of Judaism: The Unique Perspective of the Bavli on Conversion and the Construction of Jewish Identity* (Brill, 2017); *Negotiating Identities: Conflict, Conversion, and Consolidation in Early Judaism and Christianity (200 B.C.E.–600 C.E.)*, ed. Karin Hedner Zetterholm, Anders Runesson, Cecilia Wassén, and Magnus Zetterholm (Fortress Press, 2022).

15. See especially David Malkiel, *Reconstructing Ashkenaz: The Human Face of Franco-German Jewry, 1000–1250* (Stanford University Press, 2008); Tartakoff, *Conversion, Circumcision*; Tartakoff, *Between Christian and Jew*; Ephraim Kanarfogel, *Brothers from Afar*.

16. For a survey of this literature see Miriam Bodian, "The Reformation and the Jews," in *Rethinking European Jewish History*, ed. Jeremy Cohen and Moshe Rosman (Liverpool University Press, 2009), 112–132. For a more detailed and recent survey for Spain, see Miriam Bodian, "Introduction: Cultural and Religious Boundary-Crossing

in Early Modern Spain," *Jewish History* 35, nos. 3–4 (2021): 229–239. For an original European-wide analysis of interconfessional realities, see Benjamin Kaplan, *Divided by Faith: Religious Conflict and the Practice of Toleration in Early Modern Europe* (Harvard University Press, 2007).

17. For a collection dealing with Iberian notions of "blood," see *Race and Blood in the Iberian World*, ed. María Elena Martínez, Max-Sebastián Hering Torres, and David Nirenberg (Verlag, 2012).

18. See Don Seeman, *One People, One Blood: Ethiopian-Israelis and the Return to Judaism* (Rutgers University Press, 2009); Yulia Egorova, "Redefining the Converted Jewish Self: Race, Religion, and Israel's Bene Menashe," *American Anthropologist* 117, no. 3 (2015): 493–505; Naomi Leite, *Unorthodox Kin: Portuguese Marranos and the Global Search* (University of California Press, 2017); Michal Kravel-Tovi, *When the State Winks: The Performance of Jewish Conversion in Israel* (Columbia University Press, 2017).

19. Leite, *Unorthodox Kin*, 126.

20. See Jennifer Thompson's study of intermarried couples (not involving converts), *Jewish on Their Own Terms: How Intermarried Couples Are Changing American Judaism* (Rutgers University Press, 2013), 84–111.

Selected Bibliography

Bodian, Miriam. *Hebrews of the Portuguese Nation: Conversos and Community in Early Modern Amsterdam*. Indiana University Press, 1997.

Carlebach, Elisheva. *Divided Souls: Converts from Judaism in Germany, 1500–1750*. Yale University Press, 2008.

Cohen, Shaye. *The Beginnings of Jewishness: Boundaries, Varieties, Uncertainties*. University of California Press, 1999.

Ellenson, David, and Daniel Gordis. *Pledges of Jewish Allegiance: Conversion, Law, and Policymaking in Nineteenth- and Twentieth-Century Orthodox Responsa*. Stanford University Press, 2012.

Endelman, Todd. "Gender and Conversion Revisited." In *Gender and Jewish History*, edited by Marion Kaplan and Deborah Dash Moore. Indiana University Press, 2011.

Endelman, Todd. *Leaving the Jewish Fold: Conversion and Radical Assimilation in Modern Jewish History*. Princeton University Press, 2015.

Hayes, Christine. *Gentile Impurities and Jewish Identities: Intermarriage and Conversion from the Bible to the Talmud*. Oxford University Press, 2002.

Kertzer, David. *The Kidnapping of Edgardo Mortara*. Alfred Knopf, 1997.

Kravel-Tovi, Michal. *When the State Winks: The Performance of Jewish Conversion in Israel*. Columbia University Press, 2018.

Maor, Nicole, and David Ellenson, "'Who is a Convert?'—The Law of Return and the Legality of Reform and Conservative Conversions in Israel." *Israel Studies* 27, no. 2 (2022): 24–40.

Mulsow, Martin, and Richard Popkin, eds., *Secret Conversions to Judaism in Early Modern Europe*. Brill, 2004.

Nirenberg, David. "Mass Conversion and Genealogical Mentalities: Jews and Christians in Fifteenth-Century Spain." *Past & Present* 174 (2002): 3–41.

Parfitt, Tudor and Netanel Fisher, eds., *Becoming Jewish: New Jews and Emerging Jewish Communities in a Globalized World*. Cambridge Scholars Publishing, 2016.

Rambo, Lewis, and Charles Farhadian, eds. *The Oxford Handbook of Religious Conversion*. Oxford University Press, 2014.

Sagi, Avi, and Zvi Zohar. *Transforming Identity: The Ritual Transition from Gentile to Jew—Structure and Meaning*. A&C Black, 2007.

Schainker, Ellie. *Confessions of the Shtetl: Converts from Judaism in Imperial Russia, 1817–1906*. Stanford University Press, 2016.

Şişman, Cengiz. *The Burden of Silence: Sabbatai Sevi and the Evolution of the Ottoman-Turkish Dönmes*. Oxford University Press, 2015.

Yisraeli, Yosi and Yaniv Fox, eds. *Contesting Inter-Religious Conversion in the Medieval World*. Routledge, 2017.

Index

About the Author

MIRIAM BODIAN is professor of history emerita at the University of Texas at Austin. She has published widely in the fields of post-Expulsion Sephardic Jewry and the Jews in Reformation Europe. Her books *Hebrews of the Portuguese Nation*, which received two national book prizes, and *Dying in the Law of Moses* dealt extensively with issues around forced conversion.